THE WIT & WISDOM OF
GOLF

First edition (as *The Wit & Wisdom of Golf*)
©2005 House of Raven

This edition published in 2011 by Prion
An imprint of
Carlton Books Limited
20 Mortimer
London W1T 3JW

Typeset in Minion Pro and Frutiger 55
First edition design: David Coventon

ISBN: 978-1-85375-848-5

Printed in China

THE WIT & WISDOM OF
GOLF

**More than 800 amusing, enlightening
and downright bitter quotations**

PRION

Contents

• There are over 800 quotes in this collection. Each quote that appears is numbered (i.e.•123). These numbers run sequentially throughout the book. Use the index at the back to find players of, or commentators on, the game of golf. The index is listed in alphabetical order by surname.

• Both American and English spellings have been used throughout the book as appropriate.

For everyone who has ever shouted "Be The Man"
when somebody drives off at a golf tournament.
GROW UP.

There is no record of exactly when and where golf was first played, but we know that it is an old game. Early town records speak of banning orders and demands for the game to be forbidden on the Sabbath. Formal competitive golf was established in the Victorian era, and the first Open Championship was played in 1860 and won by Willie Park.

The Americans adopted the sport with zeal, and the first US open took place in 1895. By the 1920's, the great American trio of Hagen, Jones and Sarazen were dominating the major championships.

Golf is a game with a shady past. Its actual birth is shrouded in mystery. No one is quite certain when or where it drew its first tortured breath.

Will Grimsley •1

Unlike many sports, golf does not enjoy the privilege of knowing its exact birthright.

Ian Morrison •2

It is a hopeless endeavour to unite the contrarieties of spring and winter; it is unjust to claim the privileges of age, and retain the playthings of childhood.

Samuel Johnson. It is often falsely claimed that he was describing golf. •3

Of this diversion the Scots are so fond, that, when the weather will permit, you may see a multitude of all ranks, from the senator of justice to the lowest tradesmen, mingled together, in their shirts, and following the balls with utmost eagerness.

Tobias Smollett •4

It may be said especially that mankind has always displayed a uniform craving for the pastime of hitting a ball with a stick. With the savage races, an enemy's head has taken the place of the ball, but the principle is still the same.

Scotia on golf, 1886 •5

As a test of nerve, skill and temper, it seems to me to require a deal of beating, while its health promoting attendances are indisputable.

Carlton Dawe, 1907 •6

The game of golf fulfils the axioms laid down for a perfect exercise or walk with an object.

James Cantlie, Scottish physician •7

Excessive golfing dwarfs the intellect. Nor is this to be wondered at when we consider that the more fatuously vacant the mind is, the better for play. It has been observed that absolute idiots play the steadiest.

Walter Simpson, 1887 •8

Unlike the other Scotch game of whisky drinking, excess in it is not injurious to health.

Sir Walter Simpson •9

The golfer is essentially a hero worshipper; and not only is he a hero worshipper but he has faith in the methods of his heroes, a faith that is touching. …he has not a doubt that, by adopting the methods of his heroes, he will join the demigods on the Olympian heights.

Horace Hutchinson 1900 •10

Golf is deceptively simple, endlessly complicated. A child can play it well, and a grown man can never master it.

Robert Forgan, 1899 •11

There is no reason… why golf should not be begun as soon as one can walk and continued as long as one can walk.

Lord Arthur Balfour •12

Golf has robbed old age of its regrets, for it can be played from the cradle to the grave.
Gustav Kobbe •13

Golf keeps the heart young and the eyes clear.
Andrew Kirkaldy •14

Golf is more exacting than racing, cards, speculation or matrimony. *Arnold Haultain, 1910* •15

Don't worry about your caddie. He may be an irritating little wretch, but for eighteen holes he is your caddie. *Arnold Haultain, 1910* •16

All you've got is your bag carriers now. All they can do is give the golfer a weather report — not the right club.
Alfie, a seasoned caddie, at Turnberry in 1977 •17

Indeed, the highest pleasure of golf may
be that on the fairways and far from all
the pressures of commerce and rationality, we
can feel immortal for a few hours.

Colman McCarthy •18

A decision of the court decided that the game of golf may be played on a Sunday, not being a game within the view of the law, but being a form of moral effort. *Stephen Leacock* •19

In competitions, during gunfire or while bombs are falling, players may take cover without penalty for ceasing play.[20]

Shrapnel and/or bomb splinters on the fairways, or in bunkers within a club's length of a ball, may be moved without penalty and no penalties shall be incurred if a ball is thereby caused to move accidentally.[21]

A player whose stroke is affected by the simultaneous explosion of a bomb may play another ball from the same place. Penalty — one stroke. [22]

*Three of the Special Wartime Rules at
the Richmond Golf Club in Surrey*

The best way to build a golf course is to start 200 years ago. *Peter Dobereiner* •23

Golf is a good walk spoiled.

Mark Twain •24

They say golf is like life, but don't believe them.
Golf is more complicated than that.

Gardner Dickinson •25

They call it golf because all the
other four letter words were taken.

Raymond Floyd •26

Golf requires only a few simple rules and regulations to guide the players in the true nature of its sporting appeal. The spirit of the game is its own referee.

Robert Harris •27

On the average, a maximum of 4.097% of the time associated with a round of golf is spent whacking the golf ball with a golf club.

Geoff Howson •28

Golf is twenty percent mechanics and technique. The other eighty percent is philosophy, humour, tragedy, romance, melodrama, companionship, camaraderie, cussedness and conversation. *Grantland Rice* •29

To play golf is the search for perfection. The seemingly endless struggle to retain the unattainable.

A.J. Dalconen •30

A passion, an obsession, a romance,
a nice acquaintanceship with trees,
sand, and water. *Bob Ryan* •31

You begin to get the idea that maybe
golf manufacturers are out of control when
you find out they're making clubs and balls
out of components used in nuclear weapons
and bullet-proof vests.

E.M. Swift •32

It is not a matter of life and death. It is not that
important. But it is a reflection of life, and so
the game is an enigma wrapped in a mystery
impaled on a conundrum.

Peter Alliss with his usual bag of mixed metaphors and borrowed aphorisms •33

The sport of kings, the pastime of the people, the game of the old and the young, golf can be played by all. All classes may mingle, all shapes and sizes may adapt themselves, the light weight has an equal chance with the heaviest, all play on the same ground on equal footing. Golf has become international and universal.

Robert Harris, 1953. A sentiment not shared by the committee's of the majority of the world golf clubs. •34

If you call on God to improve the results of a shot whilst it is still in motion, you are using an outside agency and are subject to appropriate penalties under the rules of golf.

Henry Longhurst •35

There's something intrinsically therapeutic about choosing to spend your time in a wide, open park-like setting that non-golfers can never truly understand. *Charles Rosin in Northern Exposure* •36

No game designed to be played
with the aid of personal servants by
right-handed men who can't even
bring along their dogs can
be entirely good for the soul.

Bruce McCall, The Case Against Golf •37

Far and Sure.

The motto of the Royal & Ancient •38

It is the native dignity which outweighs all factitious advantages; his the pleasant demeanour, courteous without servility, independent without aggression, which affects favourably to all.

H. Everard on Old Tom Morris •39

He was the best golfer who ever addressed himself to a ball.

Robert Clark, on Young Tom Morris, 1880 •40

The golfer will not do good work unless he is fed.
And it is real, good, hard work that he has to do,
work that will need a stout heart to do it.

Horace Hutchinson, 1899 •41

Never was more fallacious advice given the unsuspecting
golfing community, and that from one of the best golfers
and best men that ever played the game. This advice has
ruined many a man's game. *Charles Blair McDonald, 1928,*
refutes Hutchinson's advice •42

No game demands more scientific accuracy
than golf, and there is no game in which shots
that are not well played more surely meet with a
just punishment. *James Braid, 1901* •43

It is extremely unlikely that the disasters that occur to every beginner
are in the least degree the fault of the clubs and the player will only get
himself into a quandary if he allows himself to think so.

James Braid, 1906 •44

Never allow yourself to wonder, and never play to the gallery. It is the steady game that brings the player to the fore. *J. H. Taylor, five-time winner of the British Open* •45

It is due to him, more than any other man, that the profession has climbed so far from its old unsatisfactory condition. He is a natural speaker, a natural fighter, a natural leader who would have made his mark in any walk of life. *Bernard Darwin on J.H. Taylor* •46

The object of a bunker or trap is not only to punish a physical mistake, to punish lack of control, but also to punish pride and egotism.

Charles Blair McDonald •47

If I had my way, I've never let the sand be raked. Instead, I'd run a herd of elephants through the bunkers every morning.

Charles Blair McDonald •48

He smiles as he plays, but it is not a broad smile, just a faint flicker over his features, it is what you might call the Vardonic smile. He was never a worrier, or a recounter of lost strokes. Nothing ruffled him.

Andrew Kirkaldy •49

Moderation is essential in all things, Madam, but never in my life have I failed to beat a teetotaller. *Harry Vardon* •50

The advent of the rubber ball was instrumental in creating an entirely different method of striking the object… I hold the firm opinion that from this date the essential attitude toward accuracy was completely lost sight of. This was the start
of the craze for length and still more length.

Harry Vardon •51

When practising, use the club that gives you the most trouble, and do not waste your time in knocking the ball about with a tool that gives you the most satisfaction and with which you rarely make a bad stroke.

Harry Vardon •52

Never saw one who was worth a damn.

Harry Vardon on left-handers •53

You can't always be playing well when it counts.
You'll never win golf tournaments until you learn to
score well when you're playing badly.

Jim Barnes, winner of the
British Open in 1925 •54

The right way to play golf is to go up and hit the bloody thing.

George Duncan •55

He generally turned out in a deerstalker hat and an old
teddy bear coat secured around the waist by string which
reduced him to something like a quarter swing.

Peter Ryde on John Morrison, golfer
and all-round sportsman •56

To play good golf rests entirely on the ability to find the back of the ball with the club head square. *Henry Cotton in 1980* •57

I have seen the champions come and go like short lived daffodils and bluebells.

Henry Cotton 58

Once again Hagen has shown that concentration counts, and that a man who refuses to smoke during a round has the advantage over his rivals who cannot keep their pipe or cigarettes for other times.

Arthur Lee on Walter Hagen
in The Guardian, 1924 •59

Which one of you is going to be runner-up?

Walter Hagen, before the
1925 US PGA (attrib) •60

No one remembers who came second.

Walter Hagen •61

When I used to see him come to the clubhouse in the morning wearing a tuxedo, I knew we were in for a bad day. *Leggy Ahern, Walter Hagen's caddie* •62

I never wanted to be millionaire; I just wanted to live like one.

Walter Hagen •63

If you three putt the first green, they'll never remember it. But if you three putt the 18th, they'll never forget it. *Walter Hagen* •64

I expect to make seven mistakes a round. Therefore, when I make a bad shot, I don't worry about it. It's just one of those seven.
Walter Hagen •65

Give me a man with big hands and big feet and no brains and I'll make a golfer out of him.
Walter Hagen •66

Never hurry, never worry, and always remember to smell the flowers along the way. *Walter Hagen* •67

I found a lot of fun playing golf and met a lot of people. I met kings and queens. Golf has always been good to me, and I hope I did a little to help golf.

Walter Hagen •68

Before Hagen broke down the walls of prejudice, a professional golfer had no standing whatever.

Gene Sarazen •69

Golf has never had a showman like him. All the professionals who have a chance to go after the big money today should say a silent thanks to Walter each time they stretch a check between their fingers.

Gene Sarazen on Walter Hagen •70

He took to thinking about it. That is a thing that has almost got to happen to any good young golfer at some time, and occasionally the young golfer is never so good again afterwards. The first careless rapture of hitting, the splendid confidence are never satisfactorily replaced.

Bernard Darwin. He was talking specifically about Gene Sarazen. •71

The fact was that Hagen, Jones and I all had weaknesses in the sand although Haig compensated by chipping from traps most of the time. *Gene Sarazen* •72

One might as well attempt to describe the smoothness of the wind as to paint a clear picture of his swing.

Grantland Rice on
Bobby Jones •73

Don't worry about par. The practice of printing par figures is literally a mental hazard. *Bobby Jones* •74

It is nothing new or original to say that golf is played one stroke at the time. But it took me many years to realise it.

Bobby Jones •75

If I needed advice from my caddie, he'd be hitting the shots and I'd be carrying the bag.

Bobby Jones •76

I have never felt so lonely as on the golf course in the midst of the championship with thousands of people around.

Bobby Jones •77

If you keep shooting par at them, they all crack sooner or later.

Bobby Jones •78

Every golfer worthy of the name should have some acquaintance with the principles of golf course design, not only for the betterment of the game, but for his own selfish enjoyment.

Bobby Jones •79

I retired from competition at 28, the same age as Bobby Jones. The difference was that Jones retired because he beat everybody. I retired because I couldn't beat anybody.

Charles Price •80

The greatest golfer in the world, being introduced by the worst one. *James Walker, Mayor of New York, introduces Bobby Jones* •81

Jones had the best that life could offer and took it with great grace, and then he had the worst and took it in the same way. *Herbert Warren Wind on the affliction that condemned Bobby Jones to a wheelchair* •82

Golf has grown in stature as a spectator sport. Once the preserve of the gentry, a huge increase in the number of courses and greater TV exposure has seen the game transcend those barriers. Golf coaches emerged in their thousands as the public battled with the peculiarities of this complex game. Standards improved, and the courses became ever more devilish and demanding to resist the long-hitting, well-equipped modern pros.

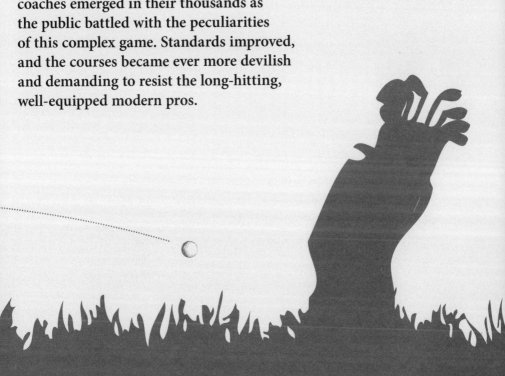

The golf ball may represent the flight of imagination but the driver reflects the baser instincts of man, the animalistic passion to dominate. I am totally addicted to my driver. Its bombs away, bombs away, bombs away.

Mac O'Grady •83

An expert player will send the ball an amazing distance at one stroke, and each player follows his ball upon an open heath, and he who strikes it in fewest strokes into a hole wins the game.

William Guthrie, 1774 •84

I can airmail the golf ball
but sometimes I don't put
the right address on it.

Jim Dent, a famous big hitter •85

Hit it hard. It will
land somewhere.

Mark Calcavecchia •86

There are no short hitters on the tour any more – just long and unbelievably long.

Sam Snead •87

If he ever grows up, he'll hit the ball 2,000 yards.

Lyle on the diminutive Ian Woosnam •88

When you're little and you hit the ball a long way, they love it. There's always some big guys around if you're looking for one. There's not many of us littles.

Ian Woosnam •89

She doesn't yell fore, she yells lift off. You don't watch the ball, you track it. An unidentified flying object entering orbit.

Jim Murray on the power of Laura Davies •90

That's fine, but I hit my putts as long as my drives.

Laura Davies placed one praise for her fearsome driving •91

If Laura used a driver off the tee and kept it in the fairway, the rest of us would be playing for second most of the time.

Nancy López •92

A mullet par excellence, big, blond and deeply unfashionable… an all-American mission statement that said I'm from Arkansas and I don't give a shit.

*Gavin Newston in **John Daly: The Biography*** •93

It's great to see. He's like every 15 and 16-year-old kid. He just rears back and hits it as far as he can and if he can find it, he's okay.

Craig Stadler on John Daly •94

John certainly gives it a

Nobody cares if John Daly shoots 80. They just want to see him hit a ball.

Gene Sarazen •95

His driving is unbelievable.
I don't go that far on my holidays.

Ian Baker-Finch on John Daly •96

good hit, doesn't he?

Nick Faldo on John Daly •97

If God had wanted man to play golf he would have given him an elbowless left arm, short asymmetrical legs with side-hinged knees, and a trapezoid rib cage from which diagonally jutted a two-foot neck topped by a three-eyed head. *Alan Coren* •98

Golf instruction books can be immensely valuable to the novice. What you do is balance it on top of your head and then swing the club as hard as you can. Once you have mastered the art of taking the full vicious swing without dislodging the book, you can play golf. *Peter Dobereiner* •99

Golf is an awkward set of bodily contortions designed to produce a graceful result. *Tommy Armour* •100

Inside each and every one of us is our one, true authentic swing. Something we were born with. Something that's ours and ours alone. Something that can't be learned... something that's got to be remembered.

Will Smith as Bagger Vance in
The Legend of Bagger Vance •101

A bad attitude is worse than a bad swing.

Payne Stewart •102

Like an octopus falling out of a tree.
David Feherty on the swing of US pro, Jim Furyk •103

The golfers' left side must be the dominant part of the swing. This is the only way to get maximum power and accuracy. If the right side takes over, there is no golf swing. *Kathy Whitworth, LPGA star* •104

Let the ball get in the way of the swing, instead of making the ball the object. *Jack Burke Sr* •105

First you teach a golfer to hook the ball by using his hands and arms properly. Then you teach him how to take the hook away by using his body and legs properly.

Harvey Penick •106

You don't hit anything on the backswing, so why rush it?

Doug Ford, winner of the Masters, 1957 •107

A golf swing is a collection of corrected mistakes.

Carol Mann, LPGA tour player •108

Dividing the swing into its parts is like dissecting a cat. You'll have blood and guts and bones all over the place. But you won't have a cat. *Ernest Jones* •109

Golf swings are like snowflakes: there are no two exactly alike.

Peter Jacobsen •110

You can buy a country but you can't buy a golf swing. It's not on the shelf. *Gene Sarazen* •111

As far as swing and techniques are concerned, I don't know diddly squat. When I'm playing well, I don't even take aim. *Fred Couples* •112

To watch a first-class field drive off must convince everyone that a golf ball can be hit in many ways.

Henry Cotton •113

Reverse every natural instinct you have and do just the opposite of what you're inclined to do and you will probably come very close to having a perfect golf swing.

Ben Hogan •114

The golf swing is like a suitcase into which we are trying to pack one too many items

John Updike •115

In using the word rhythm I am not speaking of the swing. The rhythm I have reference to here could also be described as the order of procedure. Walter Hagen was probably the greatest exponent of the kind of rhythm I have in mind to play golf.

Ben Hogan •116

Ben Hogan just knows something about hitting the golf ball the rest of them don't know. *Mike Souchak* •117

Being left-handed is a big advantage. No one knows enough about your swing to mess you up with advice.

Bob Charles •118

Watching him can be almost hypnotic. Beauty is an ephemeral quality; rarely in a golfer has it been more constantly expressed. *Pat Ward Thomas on Gene Littler* •119

There's only so much stuff in the golf swing. We are not reinventing the wheel here.

David Leadbetter takes umbrage at the suggestion that his golfing theory simply copied Mac O'Grady •120

Swing easy, hit hard.

Julius Boros •121

When it's breezy, hit it easy.

David Love III •122

When a pro hits it to the right, it's called a fade. When an amateur hits it to the right, it's called a slice.

Peter Jacobsen •123

The practice ground is an evil place. It's full of so-called coaches waiting to pounce. You can see them waiting to dish their mumbo-jumbo. To hell with coaches. *Ernie Els* •124

I think he is very mechanical. Hogan was mechanical. The mechanical golfer – and Faldo and may be the exception – is probably going to get beat by a feel player.

Jack Nicklaus on Nick Faldo •125

Ian Woosnam has got a beautiful swing. There's nothing mechanical about Woosnam at all and he's about as smooth and flowing a player as I have seen in a long time.

Jack Nicklaus •126

My golf swing is a bit like ironing a shirt. You get one side smoothed out, turn it over and there is a big wrinkle on the other side. Then you iron that one out, turn it over and there is yet another wrinkle.

Tom Watson, on struggling to find rhythm •127

Only one golfer in a thousand grips the clubs lightly enough.

Johnny Miller •128

Well, I tend to think of the golf swing as a poem. …The critical opening phrase of this poem will always be the grip, which the hands unite to form a single unit by the simple overlap of the little finger. Lowly and slowly the clubhead is led back. Pulled into position not by the hands, but by the body which turns away from the target shifting weight to the right side without shifting balance. Tempo is everything; perfection unobtainable as the body coils down at the top of the swing. There's a slight hesitation. A little nod to the gods. ….And now the weight begins shifting back to the left pulled by the powers inside the earth. It's alive, this swing, a living sculpture! And down through contact, always down, striking the ball crisply, with character. A tuning fork goes off in your heart and your balls. Such a pure feeling is the well-struck golf shot.

Kevin Costner as Roy McAvoy in Tin Cup •129

The one-iron is almost unplayable. You keep it in your bag the way you keep a Dostoevsky novel in your bookcase — with the vague notion that you will try it some day. In the meantime, it impresses your friends. *Tom Scott* •130

I've heard people say my swing's not perfect, and I know that. But golf's a natural sport, very sensitive. It's played a lot by feel. I don't care if my swing is too flat. If it works, I don't have to change it.

Sergio Garcia •131

You may be a princess but if you hold the club like that you will always be a hooker.

John Jacobs to Princess Lillian of Belgium (attrib) •132

Serenity is knowing your worst shot is still going to be good. *Johnny Miller* •133

Putting is like wisdom; partly a natural gift and partly the accumulation of experience. *Arnold Palmer* •134

There are no points for style when it comes to putting. It is getting the ball in the cup that counts.

Brian Swarbrick •135

Putting greens are to golf courses what faces are to portraits.

Charles Blair McDonald •136

Reading the green is like reading the small type in a contract. If you don't read it with painstaking care, you're likely to be in trouble. *Claude Hamilton* •137

The trouble with golf is you're only as good as your last putt.

Doug Sanders •138

Every putt is different. Your feet dictate the stroke by how they feel on the green. I just never used the same stroke on every putt.

Jack Nicklaus •139

On a putting green the mind can be a grave source of trouble. Begin to dislike the look of a putt, and the chances of holing it at once become less. *Joyce Wethered* •140

Greens near the ocean break imperceptibly toward the sea.

Ben Hogan •141

Putting is really a game within a game.

Tom Watson •142

Love and putting are mysteries
for the philosopher to solve.
Both subjects are beyond golfers.

Tommy Armour •143

Putting allows the touchy golfer two to four
opportunities to blow a gasket in the short
space of two to forty feet. *Tommy Bolt* •144

Putting affects the nerves more than anything.
I would actually get nauseated over three footers
and there were tournaments when I couldn't keep
a meal down for four days. *Byron Nelson* •145

Willie Park Junior was perhaps the deadliest putter the
game has ever known. He reckoned himself stone dead
from two yards. He would practice eight hours
a day at putting. He did much to elevate the status of
the professional golfer. *Golfers Handbook, 1975* •146

To such a perfect putter as Mr Travis, who would putt if need were with an umbrella or walking stick, doubtless there are no difficulties. *Arthur Poltow* •147

That son of a bitch was able to hole a putt over 60 feet of peanut brittle. *Lloyd Mangrum on Bobby Locke* •148

You drive for show and putt for dough.
Bobby Locke •149

Everyone examines greens, but only he knows what he's looking for.

Ben Hogan on Bobby Locke,
a formidable putter •150

That putt was so good, I could feel the baby applaud.

Donna Horton-White, on the LPGA tour,
seven months pregnant •151

My eyes go out of focus and my brain kind of goes out of a little focus too. So I don't get hung up on trying to hit anything on a perfect line. It's hard to explain.

Loren Roberts, a great putter, tries, and fails to explain his touch on the green •152

There is nothing so demoralising as missing a short putt. *Bobby Jones* •153

I always thought with my distance, Majors would be the easiest tournaments for me to win. I never realised how important putting was, and how mentally hard it was.

Davis Love III •154

I would like to knock it on every green and two-putt, but that's not my style of play or my style of living.

Muffin Spencer-Devlin •155

The less said about the putter the better. Here is an instrument of torture, designed by Tantalus and forged in the Devil's own smithy. *Tony Lema* •156

The man who once ruled it as smoothly as Bob Charles is presently putting more like Ray Charles.

Mark Reason on Jose-Maria Olazabal and his struggles on the greens •157

I enjoy the oohs and aahs from the gallery when I hit my drives, but I'm pretty tired of the aws and uhhs when I miss the putts.

John Daly •158

I'd chip it with a five iron before I'd use one of those things.

Ben Crenshaw on belly putters •159

I don't care what it looks like. We don't get paid for looking good. We get paid for getting the job done.

Bernhard Langer defends his use of a broom handle putter •160

Once you've had 'em, you've got 'em.

Henry Longhurst, on the yips •161

In my humble opinion, St Andrews is the most fascinating golf course I have ever played. There is always a way at St Andrews, although it is not always the obvious way, and in trying to find it, there is more to be learned on this British course than in playing a hundred ordinary American golf courses. *Bobby Jones* •162

In the homeland of golf, Scots played for centuries on terrain that was entirely natural. These natural links of Scotland form the foundation of the practice of golf architecture even today. *Geoffrey Cornish* •163

The older inhabitants of St Andrews may be indifferent to catastrophes, but all of them are golfers bound together in one common enthusiasm for the game. It is talked of, thought of, practised by all.

Joyce Wethered •164

This place is the very soul of golf.
You have to use your imagination.
I always enjoyed being here.

Jose-Maria Olazabal, on St Andrew's •165

It's the great original; it's positive,
rewarding, inspiring and exciting.

Peter Thomson on the old course at St Andrews •166

If there is one tiny part of your game that is
not quite right, the great course will find it
out, no matter how hard you try to hide it.

Peter Thomson, on St Andrews •167

Until you play it, St Andrews
looks like the sort of real estate you
couldn't give away. *Sam Snead* •168

St Andrews? I feel like I'm back visiting an old grandmother. She's crotchety and eccentric but also elegant. Anyone who doesn't fall in love with her has no imagination. *Tony Lema* •169

St Andrews will employ every means to deceive, flatter, cajole or dragoon you into loving it, and into admitting its mastery of you. *Patric Dickinson* •170

This course is set up perfectly to destroy a golf swing.

Peter Oosterhuis on St Andrews •171

The Road hole, the 17th, is the most famous and infamous hole. As a planner and builder of golf holes worldwide, I have no hesitation in allowing that if one built such a hole today you would be sued for incompetence. *Peter Thomson* •172

For history and tradition there is nowhere like it in the world, but I don't think it's the fairest course.

Lee Westwood •173

My most common mistake at St Andrews is turning up.

Mark James •174

When it blows here, even the seagulls walk.

Nick Faldo, on St. Andrews •175

St Andrews never impressed me at all. I wondered how it got such a reputation. The only reason could be on account of its age.

Bill Mehlhorn, one of many Americans who have moaned about the old course after playing badly there •176

They are the same people who knock the pyramids because they don't have elevators.

Jim Ferree, on players who complain about St. Andrews •177

Maybe we Americans should come and look at this course, considering the crap we are building today.

Curtis Strange, on St. Andrews •178

The ideal golf course is one that will test all golfers equally according to their respective abilities, and at the same time give an equal amount of pleasure. *W.H. Fowler* •179

A championship course is not a championship course until a championship has been played upon it. *Michael Bonallack, secretary of the R&A, states the obvious* •180

I have always loved the isolation of the early mornings on golf courses. Everything smells clean and fresh and the grass squeaks underfoot.

Dexter Westrum •181

A good golf course makes you want to play so badly you hardly have time to change your shoes.

Ben Crenshaw •182

All truly great golf courses have an almost supernatural finishing hole, by way of separating the chokers from the strokers. *Charles Price* •183

Anyone who criticises a golf course is like a person invited to a house for dinner who, on leaving, tells the host that the food was lousy. *Gary Player* •184

Carnoustie Golf Club, Scotland: a good swamp, spoiled.

You were saying, Gary? •185

SARAZEN LICKS POSTAGE STAMP

*Newspaper headline after Gene Sarazen scored a hole-in-one
at Royal Troon's famous eighth hole* •186

It looks as though a squad of Marines ought to be raising a flag over it.

*Charles Price on the raised green of
the second hole at Pine Valley* •187

I say, do you chaps try to play this hole, or do you simply photograph it and go on?

*Eustace Storey, British Walker Cup player, on seeing the
beautiful, but demanding second hole at Pine Valley* •188

In all my travels, I do not think I've seen a more beautiful landscape. This is as thrilling as Versailles or Fontainebleau. *Lord Thomas on Pine Valley* •189

It's a 300 acre unplayable lie.

Jim Murray on Pebble Beach •190

If he takes the option of dropping behind the point where the ball rests, keeping in line with the pin, his nearest drop is Honolulu.

Jimmy Demaret, as Arnold Palmer looks for a drop on the 17th at Pebble Beach •191

No.9 at Pebble Beach: this hole is harder than trigonometry.

Hubert Green •192

I don't think Pebble Beach will ever be sold to foreign investors. That would be un-American.

Dave Marr. It was. To the Japanese. •193

Eighty acres and a few cows. They ruined a good farm when they built this course.

Dave Hill on Hazeltine, in 1970 •194

This course is not like anything in Scotland or Ireland. It's like something on Mars.

David Feherty on Kiawah Island, venue for the 1991 Ryder Cup •195

It's so long that figuring distances on some holes, you have to reckon in the curvature of the Earth.

David Feherty, on Crooked Stick •196

I fell violently in love with Cypress Point. But I was so furious because I was so besotted with the beauty of it that I just couldn't hit a golf ball.

Enid Wilson •197

You don't need a roadmap for this one, you need a passport.

US pro, Jay Cronley, on the 614 yard fifth hole at Southern Hills, Tulsa •198

Muirfield without a wind is like a lady undressed. No challenge.

Tom Watson •199

If I played over here four straight weeks I'd be a raving lunatic.

Tom Watson, on the frustrations of playing golf on British links courses •200

They're going to make a
lot of money when they cut
and bale the hay out there.

Payne Stewart on Carnoustie •201

The Lytham greens are harder to read than Finnegan's Wake.

Mark Reason of the Sunday Telegraph •202

I prefer it when people are
punished for missing a fairway.
This course has been set up for
tournament professionals. We
go to too many courses where
the members have just finished
playing when we turn up.

Colin Montgomerie, at Forest of Arden •203

If you can imagine a hole halfway down the bonnet of a Volkswagen beetle; and then you have to putt it from the roof.

Nick Faldo, at the Royal Melbourne in 1990 •204

A great golf hole is one which puts a question mark into the player's mind when he arrives on the tee to play it.

Mackenzie Ross •205

Every hole should be a demanding par and a comfortable bogey.
Robert Trent Jones •206

The hazards and bumps on the course are there to offer a challenge to the skill, courage and philosophy of the player who suffers no interference in his game except from nature. The geography of the course, the temper of the elements, the quality of his courage and the unevenness of his temperament are the obstacles to be overcome. *Robert Harris* •207

Hazards are like spices that a designer sprinkles on a course to give it flavour.

Robert Trent Jones •208

There is no such thing as a misplaced bunker. Regardless of where a bunker may be, it is the business of the player to avoid it. *Donald Ross* •209

The creator of golf holes must not only possess imagination but a keen appreciation of the offerings of nature, and the art of landscaping must be aligned closely with that of the architect. *A.W. Tillinghast* •210

The man who hates golfers is what they call me. They couldn't be more wrong; I design holes that are fun to play.

Course designer Robert Trent Jones •211

The ardent golfer would play
Mount Everest if somebody
would put a flag stick on top.

Pete Dye, golf course designer •212

[Designers] don't build courses for people.
They build monuments to themselves.

George Archer •213

Golf is not a fair game,
so why build a fair course?

Peter Dye •214

What a beautiful place a golf course is. From the meanest country pasture to the Pebble Beaches and St Andrewses of the world, a golf course is to me holy ground. I feel God in the trees and grass and flowers, in the rabbits and the birds and the squirrels, in the sky and the water. I feel that I am home.

Harvey Penick •215

The individual nature of the game
means the truly great players bestride
the championships with an aura rarely
found in team sports. Golf, as is well
documented, does not yield the most
athletic-looking stars, but the combination
of power, co-ordination and touch needed
to be a champion is a rare thing.

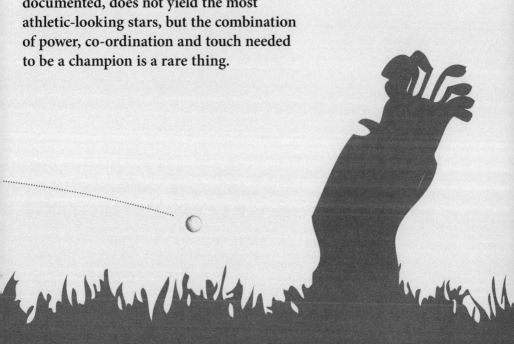

Snead was the carefree hillbilly, everybody's pal, a kind of Will Rogers of the fairways with his homely wit and hayseed yarns. *Alfred Wright* •216

Watching Sam Snead practice hitting a golf ball is like watching a fish practice swimming.

John Schlee •217

Anyone who would pass up an opportunity to see Sam Snead swing a golf club at a golf ball would pull down the shades when driving past the Taj Mahal.

Jim Murray •218

Folks always painted me like something out of Li'l Abner, but I'm proud of where I was born, and proud of the folks I came from.

Sam Snead, loyal to his West Virginia roots •219

Why did you pick today to set a course record?
What the hell do you think you're doing? I'm tired.

Sam Snead, after Tommy Aaron forced a play-off in a tournament with
a last round 64. To rub it in, Aaron won the play-off. •220

They're playing
they don't have

You gotta sneak up on these holes. If you clamber and clank
up on 'em, they're liable to turn around and bite you.

Sam Snead on Oakmont Country Club •222

Playing golf is like eating.
It's something which has
to come naturally. •223

84

I loved matchplay. I would study a guy I was
playing, just like Ted Williams studied pitch-
ers. I look for a weak spot. •224

for so much money,
time to smile.

Sam Snead on the modern tour •221

These greens are so fast I have
to hold my putter over the ball
and hit it with the shadow. •225

I'm only scared of three things: lightning,
a side hill putt, and Ben Hogan. •226

Of all the hazards, fear is the worst. •227

One day you're up on cloud nine and the next day you couldn't scratch a whale's belly..228

If a lot of people gripped a knife and fork the way they do a golf club, they'd starve to death..229

Of course, he's still got it.

Dave Marr, suggesting that Sam Snead, notoriously tight with his money, still has the £500 he won for winning the British Open in 1946 •230

The road's getting shorter and narrower, but I'll play wherever the pigeons land.

Sam Snead at 81 •231

He is the most immeasurable of golf champions. ...it is partly because of the nobility he has brought to losing. And more than anything, it is true because of the pure, unmixed joy he has brought to trying.

Dan Jenkins on Arnold Palmer •232

Anybody who resents Arnold getting more attention than the rest of us doesn't deserve to use his head for more than a hat rack.

Doug Sanders •233

Golf is a way of testing ourselves while enjoying ourselves. •234

What other people may find in poetry or art museums, I find in the flight of a good drive. •235

Winning isn't everything, but wanting to is. •236

I've always had Arnold's gallery to fight, but I never had to fight Arnold. I've never forgotten that.

Jack Nicklaus on the good nature of his great rival, Arnold Palmer •237

Arnie would go for the flag from the middle of an alligator's back.

Lee Trevino •238

If ever I needed an eight foot putt, and everything I owned depended on it, I would want Arnold Palmer to putt for me. *Bobby Jones* •239

I never figured out what women
saw in him, but I'd like a case of it.

Peter Dobereiner, on Arnold Palmer, an unlikely sex symbol •240

Arnold's place in history will be as the man
who took golf from a game for the few to a
sport for the masses. He was the catalyst that
made it happen. *Jack Nicklaus* •241

Arnold Palmer is Mr Golf; he's fried chicken and apple pie. And him
putting with his hands separated is un-American. *Lee Trevino* •242

Did you read that Arnold Palmer has been talking about the
governorship of Pennsylvania? Man, I think that hip injury
must be moving up to his head. *Dave Marr* •243

You can describe my round as having moments of ecstasy and
stark raving terror. I looked like I knew what I was doing at
times and at other times I looked like a 20-handicap player.
Arnold Palmer at the 1968 US PGA •244

I love Arnie to death but it's time for him to surrender. I know he still loves to play golf but there's no point in being out there if you shoot 83 or 84. *Mark Calcavecchia on the sad sight of Arnold Palmer floundering around Augusta in 1999* •245

Palmer and Player played superbly, but Nicklaus played a game with which I'm not familiar. *Bobby Jones* •246

It's a shame that Bob Jones isn't here. He could have saved the words he used for me in 1963 for this young man because he is certainly playing a game with which we're not familiar.

Jack Nicklaus on Tiger Woods •247

He's the only golfer I've ever seen who should be required to play with a handicap. *Bobby Jones on Jack Nicklaus* •248

I let the Bear out of his cage.

*Arnold Palmer on losing the 1962 US open
play off to Jack Nicklaus* •249

If there is one thing golf demands
above all else, it is honesty.•250

A kid grows up a lot faster on the golf course;
Golf teaches you how to behave. You start playing
with older people so that a kid who plays golf is
different from a lot of athletes in other sports
because he hasn't had his own way. He hasn't
been spoiled. •251

All athletes, when they get in pressure
situations, revert to what they know.
I don't think you are going to revert to
mechanics. I think you revert to feel.•252

I think I fail a bit less

Jack Nicklaus (attrib) •253

The longer you play, the better chance the better player has of winning.

Jack Nicklaus, on how the cream usually comes to the surface in major tournaments •254

Tournaments are won on Sunday and on the back nine. •255

When Nicklaus plays well, he wins. When he plays badly, he finishes second. When he plays terribly, he finishes third. *Johnny Miller* •256

94

han everybody else.

The guys I'll never understand are the self-confessed non-competitors; the golfers who pick up $100,000 plus a year without ever winning a tournament and go around telling the world how happy they are to finish ninth every week.•257

He plays like a beautifully proportioned field gun, automatic with perfect range.
Leonard Crawley on Jack Nicklaus •258

Golf is a better game played downhill..259

All my life I wanted to play like Jack Nicklaus, and now I do.
Paul Harvey, TV journalist, after the great man shot an 83 in the 1981 British Open •260

◯

DONE, THROUGH, WASHED UP

Atlanta Constitution in 1986 on Jack Nicklaus; he won the Masters a week later •261

If I could just putt, I might just scare somebody, maybe me.

Jack Nicklaus, sensing an opportunity to win that 1986 Masters, aged 46 •262

I kept getting tears in my eyes… I have to say to myself, hey, you've got some golf to play.

Jack Nicklaus, in the finishing strait at Augusta in 1986 •263

The older you get the stronger the wind gets and it's always in your face.

•264

I'm about as concerned as Jack would be if he read that
I was practising to compete in the Masters.

Mark MacCormack on hearing that Jack Nicklaus
had set up a sports management firm •265

I don't see Norman and Ballesteros and Faldo out there.

Jack Nicklaus, responding to Gary Player's suggestion that
winning the Senior PGA was like winning a fifth major •266

Reporter: You really know your way
around a course. What's your secret?
Jack Nicklaus: The holes are numbered.
•267

I think this is the only tournament I've ever gone into that I'm
hoping I can finish second. That would be the neat part. *Jack*
Nicklaus gets behind his son, Gary, at the 1996 US Open •268

I don't know. I've never been anyone else's son.

Gary Nicklaus' response to a crass question on how hard it is to be Jack's son •269

The boy is a genius.
If he ever learns to play
he will be unbeatable.

John Jacobs on Seve in 1976 •270

I am still young, when I'm older
there will be time to be careful.

Seve, after finishing runner-up in the 1976
British Open. He never did find time. •271

Seve – the greatest thing to come
out of Spain since a painting by Picasso
that made sense. *Dan Jenkins* •272

He goes after a golf course like a lion at a
zebra... he tries to hold its head under
the water until it stops wriggling.

Jim Murray mixing metaphors about Seve. •273

If the water is rough in Santander Bay you fight harder in the boat. You do not give up.

Seve Ballesteros, fisherman's son •274

It doesn't matter if you look like a beast before or after the hit, as long as you look like a beauty at the moment of impact..•275

God said to Faldo, as he once said to Nicklaus, "you will have skills like no other". Then he whispered to Ballesteros, as he whispered to Palmer, "but they will love you more".

Tom Callahan in The Washington Post •276

Sometimes I think the only way the Spanish people will recognise me is if I win the grand slam and then drop dead on the 18th green.

Seve Ballesteros, adored abroad, ignored at home. •277

The soles of your feet tingle as you watch and when he grins you are suddenly sharing the feeling: the pure joy of hitting the ball.

Dudley Doust on Seve Ballesteros, aged 20 •278

In the United States I'm lucky; in Europe, I'm good.

Severiano Ballesteros neatly sums up American parochialism •279

You have the hands, now play with your heart.

Roberto De Vicenzo to Seve Ballesteros in 1979.
He did, and won the British Open. •280

What came as a shock and delight was the way he kicked down the doors, he elbowed the mighty Jack Nicklaus, Hale Irwin and Tom Watson aside and plonked himself down in the seat of honour.

Peter Dobereiner on Seve winning the 1979 British Open •281

The winner, Severiano Ballesteros, chose not to use the course but preferred his own, which mainly consisted of hay fields, car parks, grandstands, dropping zones and even ladies' clothing.

Colin McLaine, speaking after Ballesteros'
British Open win at Lytham in 1979 •282

I can't understand badly and still win

Hale Irwin, on Seve in 1979 •283

Seve Ballesteros drives into territory
Daniel Boone couldn't find. *Fuzzy Zoeller* •284

Seve can have an off day and still win. But if Seve
plays well and the rest of us play well, Seve wins.
Ben Crenshaw •285

Seve still has an aura about him, even for me. There
are individuals in the world that you are around
who you can feel the energy from.
Greg Norman •286

Catching Seve is like a Chevy pickup
trying to catch a Ferrari. *Tom Kite* •287

how anyone can drive that
an Open championship.

When Jack Nicklaus told me I was playing Ballesteros, I took so many pills that I'm glad they don't have drug tests for golfers.

Fuzzy Zoeller at the 1983 Ryder Cup •288

Seve's got shots the rest of us don't even know.

Ben Crenshaw •289

The only time I talk on a golf course is to my caddie. And then only to complain when he gives me the wrong club. •290

If we were in charge, we would have far more matchplay. That is real golf. I love matchplay. •291

I look into their eyes, shake their hand, pat their back, and wish them luck, but I'm thinking, I'm going to bury you.
•292

I'd like to see the fairways more narrow. Then everybody would have to play from the rough, not just me.•293

I don't trust doctors. They are like golfers. Each one has a different answer to your problem.•294

He was our Arnold Palmer, Pele, Muhammad Ali — he was that big a name.

Colin Montgomerie on the sad death in 2011 of Severiano Ballesteros •295

But is it legitimate to call a golfer
the greatest athlete in the world?
Is it acceptable to compare him to
Muhammad Ali, Pele, Michael Jordan,
Steven Redgrave, Martina Navratilova?

Simon Barnes on the pre-eminence of Tiger Woods •296

Earl Woods has said a lot of things I don't think they're
mention or acknowledgement. Tiger Woods, of course,
is a great athlete... he's a great competitor, and his ability to
focus is tremendous. I put it right there with Michael Jordan and
myself. *Michael Johnson – Woods snr had made the preposterous claim
that had Tiger been a runner he would have beaten Johnson •297*

I don't know. I've
never played there.

*Sandy Lyle, when asked his opinion of talented newcomer,
Tiger Woods, in 1992. •298*

He's a freak of nature, worlds apart from us in every way.

Michael Campbell on Tiger Woods, long before Campbell held off a
fierce attack from Woods to win the 2005 US Open •299

He has the ability to do things no one else can do and yet has a short game where, if he makes mistakes, he can correct it. That's what's so phenomenal about him.

Jack Nicklaus on Tiger Woods •300

I don't watch him much. Sometimes he hits shots that nobody else in the world can. You have to learn to play with him and I'm fortunate to have done that.

Thomas Bjorn, and how to tame the Tiger in matchplay •301

She's our Tiger Woods.

Laura Davies on Michelle Wie. It didn't quite work out. •302

I haven't played to my full potential yet. And when that happens it will just be me and Tiger.

Then world No26 Ian Poulter in 2008; this oft-quoted tongue-in-cheek remark
was taken with absurd seriousness by the po-faced gentlemen of the press. •303

Tiger Woods has become as pervasive as the weather in the lives of all other tournament professionals. His form governs the climate of their existence. *Hugh McIlvanney* •304

You do get the feeling sometimes that the rest of us are all out here playing for second place. *Fred Couples on Tiger Woods* •305

Tiger is a great guy, probably the most professional sportsman in the world, but the intensity of his life is just ridiculous. That was really brought home to me when he explained why he loves scuba-diving so much. He said it was because the fish didn't recognise him.

Lee Westwood •306

I wouldn't want Tiger's life, even if it does bring things like a $40 million Nike contract. It's not worth it. I can go out for a drink with my mates and no one bothers me, and that's how I like it. I would never want bodyguards, all that hassle.

Lee Westwood •307

I did envisage being this successful as a player, but not all the hysteria around it off the golf course.•308

Everyone wants to give me advice. I go into the grocery store and someone tells me what I did wrong with the four-iron I hit on the 15th. •309

I don't know if you're ever finished trying to improve. As soon as you feel like you're finished, then I guess you are finished, because you've already put a limit on your ability and what you can attain. I don't think that's right. •310

I get to play golf for a living. What more can you ask for — getting paid for doing what you love?•311

I've learned to trust the subconscious. My instincts have never lied to me.•312

Surely Tiger's decision to outsource sexual services to a range of competing providers is in line with management consultancy's established best practice? Previously he had been tied to a monopoly Scandinavian supplier — with the cripplingly high social costs this usually entails. Moreover, give his wife's age, it is possible that she was on the brink of becoming a depreciating asset who needed to be moved off the balance sheet as soon as possible. ... Admittedly he could have off-shored more — to girls from low-wage economies. But the arrangement where he could have anything from nil to three girls on call at any one time allows for better load-balancing, enabling him to handle the peaks and troughs of demand better than under the previous inflexible arrangement. By sourcing girls locally, he was also reducing distribution costs and helping the environment ... while allowing him to adopt a best-of-breed approach to sexual delivery, rather than depending on a single source.

Rory Sutherland's blog in Campaign questions why Accenture, the Management Consultancy group, dropped their sponsorship of Tiger Woods in the aftermath of revelations about his sexual shenanigans. •313

I wanted to accept this trophy with dignity. But I guess that's just not my style.

Amy Alcott, on an undignified jump into the lake after winning the 1991 Dinah Shore •314

I sometimes think Sandy plays in a cloud of unconscious competence.

Peter Alliss •315

Great champions learn from past experiences, whether those be good or bad. A lot of times a guy needs to be knocked down before he gets up and fights. *Paul Azinger* •316

I don't enjoy playing video golf because there is nothing to throw.

Paul Azinger •317

Retire to what? I'm a golfer and a fisherman. I've got no place to retire to. *Julius Boros* •318

It takes a lot of guts to play this game, and by looking at Billy Casper you can tell he certainly has a lot of guts.

Gary Player on the portly Billy Casper •319

You couldn't tell whether he was on the right or left of the fairway because his ball was so close to the middle.

Dai Rees on Henry Cotton •320

I tried to pay attention and not look around so much. But there's a lot to look at. *Fred Couples* •321

To me, he's very boring. He's or in the water. He's not the best putter. He's just the best

Fred Couples on Nick Faldo •322

People are always telling me I should do one thing or another. I should change my grip or shorten my swing. I should practise more and goof around less. I shouldn't smile on Sunday – I should – I shouldn't – frankly, I don't know why they worry. It's my life – and I don't worry. *Fred Couples* •323

I had a 15th club in my bag
this week. It was Harvey Penick.
Ben Crenshaw •324

never in the trees
best driver, not the
at everything.

Ben Crenshaw hits in the woods so often he
should get an orange hunting jacket.
Tom Weiskopf •325

You look at Faldo and you have
to resist the temptation to look
at the back for the knobs.
Jim Murray on Nick Faldo. •326

I want people to say:
did you ever see Nick
Faldo play? *Nick Faldo* •327

I owe everything to golf. Where else could a guy with an IQ like mine make this much money?

Hubert Green •328

The only emotion Ben shows in defeat is surprise.

Jimmy Demaret on Ben Hogan •329

It hurts to win. In my case my stomach tightens and stays like that until it's all over. There are a lot of golfers around who in the same position suddenly blow up and put themselves out of the running. They won't admit it but deep down they almost wanted that blow up. It takes the pressure off them. *Brian Huggett* •330

Hale took off like a possessed teenager at a disco. He slapped his hands with the gallery, running round the 18th green giving low, middle and high fives.

Jack Whitaker on Hale Irwin's spectacular celebrations after holing a monster putt of the last hole to force a play-off in the 1990 US open. Irwin won the play-off. •331

I've been overcommitted and sidetracked by business and social demands and everything else that goes with being the champion.

Tony Jacklin on the consequences of winning major tournaments •332

The best feeling of all? …you are in your room on your own and you stare at the ceiling and say to yourself: By God, I beat the lot of them. I really did beat them all. That's the real moment to savour.

Tony Jacklin •333

I think any time you're in the hunt for a major championship, you learn something about yourself. *Tom Lehman* •334

If you don't enjoy pressure, you're in the wrong place.

Justin Leonard •335

Are you kidding? The only big word I know is delicatessen, and I can't even spell it.

Lloyd Mangrum's response to the idea that he should write a book •336

I played with Carol Mann when she won her first tournament and I didn't think she was going to get off the last hole. I remember she asked me if I had an air-sickness bag. She didn't even know where she was. *Judy Rankin on Carol Mann* •337

It'll be nice not to use my fake IDs any more.

Phil Mickelson, on turning 21 •338

He doesn't drink. To face that kind of pressure, week after week, you have to drink.

Ralph Kiner on the young Johnny Miller •339

I wasn't born with this ability. I had to work bloody hard to become the player I am today.

Colin Montgomerie •340

People say it is too bad that I won all those events when the prizemoney was so small, but I'm not envious. …it was fun when I played, much more fun I fancy than it is now. *Byron Nelson* •341

The only shots you can be dead sure of are those you've had already. *Byron Nelson* •342

I think he wants to be included in the glory of it all, but deep down I don't think he is totally comfortable having the last shot.
Johnny Miller on Greg Norman. Norman eventually proved Miller wrong. •343

I owe a lot to my
parents, especially my
mother and father.

Greg Norman •344

It could be worse;
I could be allergic to beer.

Greg Norman, on finding out he had an allergy to grass •345

Play every shot as if it's the first shot you're
ever going to play. The tournament starts on
the next shot you hit.

Greg Norman •346

When you're playing well, you can
hit the ball within a foot
of where you want it to land.

Greg Norman •347

You go out and play your game. Sometimes it comes out at 68 and sometimes at 74. That's not fatalism, that's golf. *Peter Oosterhuis* •348

I know now how Lawrence of Arabia must have felt after spending most of his time under the ropes and in the sand.
Craig Parry after an erratic round. He still won •349

He plays the game of golf as if he has a plane to catch; as if he were double parked and left the meter running. Guys move slower leaving hotel fires. *Jim Murray on Corey Pavin* •350

Golf is a puzzle without an answer. I've played golf for 40 years and I still haven't the slightest idea how to play.

Gary Player •351

It's a marriage. If I had to choose between my wife and my putter… well, I'd miss her.

Gary Player •352

I wear black. I loved westerns and the Cowboys always look good in black.

Gary Player •353

Playing against him, you begin hoping he'll be on grass rather than in sand. From grass you expect him to pitch the ball close. From a bunker you're afraid he'll hole it out. *Jack Nicklaus on Gary Player's uncanny ability with a sand wedge* •354

The more I practice, the luckier I get.

Gary Player •355

I still get butterflies on the first tee. I still get sweaty hands, and my heart pumps a lot going down the 18th. But I know what winning is all about now, and that's a feeling that I like.

Annika Sorenstam •356

What's scary about her is that she doesn't make mistakes. You know you've got to beat her. She's not going to crumble.

Sophie Gustafson on Annika Sorenstam •357

I think it's funny that almost all the sports writers who are always asking why Craig doesn't lose weight are heavier than he is.

Sue Stadler •358

I still hit bad shots, but it never was pretty with me. There was always a lot of snortin' and sweatin' and bitchin'. I was full of blood, sweat and tears. *Curtis Strange* •359

It means what every little boy dreams about when he plays by himself late in the afternoon. He has three or four balls; one's Hogan, one's Palmer, one's Nicklaus, the other is Strange. Ninety nine percent of the time those dreams don't come true.

Curtis Strange, with a touchingly human appreciation of winning •360

It's really hard when people are telling you how good you should be all the time; it's really hard to live up to everybody else's expectations.

Hal Sutton •361

I never heard of them before. I thought it was some kind of sunglasses.

Lanny Wadkins talking about beta-blockers •362

I hate to lose at anything, even at checkers, chess, pool, you name it. I feel if you ease up in any game it breeds a quitting attitude. *Tom Watson* •363

The person I fear most in the last two rounds is myself. *Tom Watson* •364

Wind and rain are great challenges. They separate the real golfers. Let the seas pound against the shore, let the rain pour.

Tom Watson, one of the game's greatest links players •365

I would hate to have won two world championships – the British open and the Masters – knowing I had used illegally grooved clubs.

Gary Player, never the best loser, belittles
Tom Watson for an unintentional error •366

Since Tom's clubs are illegal and he used them to win the Masters and the British Open where I came second, does it mean I am now the winner?

Jack Nicklaus takes a more light-hearted view •367

If you call personality the Battle of Hollywood stars, then yes, we do lack personality. But the personality of golf is good golf. If you want to see a comedian, you ought to tune into Saturday Night Live. *Tom Watson* •368

I was like a swan gliding on top with my legs paddling madly underneath.

Lee Westwood, on coping with the pressure of leading a tournament •369

I didn't need to finish college to know what golf was all about. All you need to know is to hit the ball, find it and hit it again until it disappears into the hole in the ground. *Fuzzy Zoeller* •370

I don't think of myself as a celebrity or superstar. I'm just an ordinary guy who makes his living in a crazy way… my only fear is that I may have to go out and get a real job.

Fuzzy Zoeller •371

Golf pros often come over as dour and unsmiling; this is an inevitable consequence of a game which demands such fierce concentration, and punishes a moment of weakness so severely. Behind the frowns and dark glasses lie some sparky characters, from the chirpy banter of Lee Trevino to the penetrating acerbity of pro-turned-pundit, David Feherty.

If you watch
a game, it's fun.
If you play at it,
its recreation.
If you work at it,
it's golf. *Bob Hope* •372

One minute you're bleeding, the next minute your haemorrhaging, the next minute you're painting the Mona Lisa. *Mac O'Grady on a typical round of golf* •373

Knickers are good for my golf game. They're cooler in hot weather because the air circulates in them and they're warmer in cold weather because they track the body heat.

*Payne Stewart explains
the rationale behind his
idiosyncratic outfits* •374

I wore slacks on the practice tee on Tuesday and everybody looked at the name on my bag to see who I was.

Payne Stewart, on life without his trademark plus-two's •375

There is no clause in the rules which says anything about Union Jack trousers and we shall not be asking Ian to change them. *Peter Dawson of the R&A on Ian Poulter's attire at the 2004 British Open* •376

Doug Sanders' outfit has been described as looking like the aftermath of a direct hit on a pizza factory. *Dave Marr* •377

Golf is not a sport. Golf is men in ugly pants, walking. *Robin Williams* •378

At dinner in a Southport hotel one night a member of our party, a slightly fey woman with a Greer Garson complex, picked up a carnation from the table decoration and sent a waiter with it to Bywaters who was sitting at a nearby table. He acknowledged it with an extravagant bow, dunked it into his claret and ate it with obvious relish.

Peter Dobereiner remembers PGA secretary, Major John Bywaters •379

You don't know what he charged me for the ride out. I'll have to win the damn thing to get back home.

Ray Floyd, after hitching a lift on
Greg Norman's private plane •380

I went to bed and I was old and washed up. I woke up a rookie. What could be better?

Ray Floyd, on turning 50 and becoming eligible for the Seniors •381

What I want is Fred Couples' face. And I want Fred Couples' body. And Fred Couples' swing. His hair... actually, I want anybody's hair. *Rocky Thompson, a pro on the senior tour* •382

Always throw clubs ahead of you. That way you don't have to waste energy going back to pick them up. *Tommy Bolt, a notoriously volatile US pro with a penchant for club throwing* •383

Flippy-wristed little college kids.

Tommy Bolt resents some of the tour's younger challengers •384

The biggest liar in the world is the golfer who claims that he plays the game merely for exercise.

Tommy Bolt •385

It doesn't matter how bad you are playing or how high you are shooting, you still have to be generous and pleasant. *Sergio García* •386

It's nice to see somebody who doesn't look like he came off a Wheaties box. He's just fun to watch. *Johnny Miller on Sergio García* •387

He has a lot of composure and talent, but he's also a fine young man. If he was a great player and a jerk, it would be different, but he's a very engaging and delightful person. *Hale Irwin on Sergio García* •388

Every golfer has a little monster in him, it's just that type of sport.

Fuzzy Zoeller •389

It just happened that the hole got in the way. I was trying to make four and I made three.

Fuzzy Zoeller explains an eagle three •390

I started drinking four years after I started playing golf. And I started playing golf when I was four. *John Daly* •391

I think they need to look at their own lives before they use that pen. I'm sure a lot of those guys in the media don't have perfect lives. *John Daly, on the media's intrusion into his private life* •392

Most people would be drunk for two days on what I have before dinner.

John Daly •393

Like a hurricane his arrival came without warning and his game spells danger wherever he plays.

David Leadbetter on John Daly •394

Woosy and I are talking about marriage. He says it's the longest relationship he's ever had. *John Daly, after partnering Ian Woosnam in all four rounds of the Masters* •395

I allowed myself to be led astray by Ian Woosnam.

Darren Gough turns up late for a test match after a night on the tiles, and blames his golfing friend •396

Some players would complain if they were playing on Dolly Parton's bedspread. *Jimmy Demaret* •397

Sammy Davis Jr hits the ball 130 yards and his jewellery goes 150.

Bob Hope •398

I refuse to play golf with
Errol Flynn. If I want to play
with a prick, I'll play with
my own. *W.C. Fields* •399

That was a great
game of golf, fellas.

Bing Crosby's last words •400

I'm the best.
I just haven't
played yet.

Muhammad Ali •401

138

I think most of the rules of golf stink. They were written by guys who can't even break a hundred.

Chi Chi Rodríguez •402

It's still embarrassing. I asked my caddie for a sand wedge, and ten minutes later he came back with a ham on rye. *Chi Chi Rodríguez, on the perils of touring the USA with a Mexican accent* •403

I played like Doug Sanders and putted like Colonel Sanders. *Chi Chi Rodríguez* •404

I don't fear death, but I sure don't like those three footers for par. *Chi Chi Rodríguez* •405

I never exaggerate.
I just remember big.
Chi Chi Rodríguez •406

Golf is the most fun you can have without taking your clothes off.
Chi Chi Rodríguez •407

The first time I played the Masters, I was so nervous I drank a bottle of rum before I teed off. I shot the happiest 83 of my life.
Chi Chi Rodríguez •408

I wouldn't follow Farrah Fawcett around here today. *Chi Chi Rodríguez, at the 1982 Masters, plagued by awful weather* •409

I never played with the Lone Ranger before.

Chi Chi Rodríguez. His partner, Orville Moody, wore a mask because he suffered from hayfever •410

The ball's got to stop somewhere, it might as well be at the bottom of the whole. *Lee Trevino adopts a positive attitude on the green* •411

You can make a lot of money out of golf. Ask any of my ex-wives.

Lee Trevino •412

I plan to win so much money this year, my caddy's gonna finish in the top 20 money winners. *Lee Trevino* •413

Rough should have high grass.
When you go bowling they don't
give you anything for landing in
the gutter, do they?

Lee Trevino •414

My swing is so bad I look like a caveman killing his lunch.

Lee Trevino •415

Columbus went around the world in 1492.
That isn't a lot of strokes when you consider
the course. *Lee Trevino* •416

I've never had a coach in
my life; when I can find
one who can beat me,
I'll listen. *Lee Trevino* •417

Practising is my medication. Some golfers like to fish and others read. I like to hit golf balls. *Lee Trevino* •418

Nobody but you and your caddie care what you do out there, and if your caddie is betting against you, he doesn't care either.

Lee Trevino •419

If God wanted you to putt cross-handed, he would have made your left arm longer.

Lee Trevino •420

Norman makes the rest of us look like we're hitting tennis balls. *Lee Trevino* •421

At one time I had fifteen clubs. When we left the fifth green, Nicklaus couldn't find his putter. He had put it in my bag. I told him I'd take the two shot penalty if he didn't use the putter for the rest of the round.

Lee Trevino after a round with
Jack Nicklaus at the USPGA •422

I'm sorry Lee lost, he's such a great guy, but I wouldn't let my wife beat me if I could help it.

Lee Trevino after beating
Lee Elder in a play-off •423

I may buy the Alamo and give it back to Mexico.

Lee Trevino ponders what to do with his record winnings in 1968 •424

It's like diving off a high board
or skiing down a steep mountain.
It's always easier to do something
once you've done it.

Lee Trevino, having won the
US Open the second time •425

This is my driver, man. If he goes,
I go too. I can drive out the same
way I drove in. *Lee Trevino, when an official tried to*
prevent his black driver entering the
parking area at Augusta National •426

I adore the game of golf. I won't ever retire. I'll play until I
die. Then I want them to roll me into a bunker, cover me
with sand and make sure nobody's ball lands in there for
awhile. *Lee Trevino* •427

One of the nice things about the Senior Tour is that we can take a cart and cooler. If your game is not going well, you can always have a picnic. *Lee Trevino* •428

I just wish he would get out on the Seniors' tour and get away from the rest of us other fellows. *Lanny Wadkins, after 44-year-old Lee Trevino wins the US PGA* •429

I'm sorry. I hope I wasn't in the way.

Lee Trevino, to Thomas Bjorn, after taking 80 in the 2000 British Open •430

Do remember, Finch-Hatton, that you are playing for your side and not for yourself. *Varsity match spectator to the American Oxford captain, Denys Finch-Hatton* •431

And do remember that you are playing for neither.

Finch-Hatton's response •432

The pleasure derived from hitting the ball dead centre on the club is comparable only to one of two other pleasures that come to mind at the moment.

Dinah Shore •433

I would rather play Hamlet on Broadway with no
rehearsal than tee off at Pebble Beach on television.

Jack Lemmon, legendary golfing enthusiast (and Muppet) •434

Jack Lemmon is not one of those actors who will
bore you to death discussing acting. He'd rather
bore you to death discussing golf. *George Cukor* •435

Titleist has offered me a big contract not to play its balls. *Bob Hope* •436

Actually, I am a golfer. That is my real
occupation. I never was an actor; ask
anybody, particularly the critics.

Victor Mature •437

I've got a feeling for the game of golf. I did very
well on the course in Skegness, until I got stuck
in one of the little wooden windmills.

Leonard Rossiter as Rigsby in Rising Damp •438

On one hole I'm like Arnold Palmer, and on the next like Lili Palmer. *Sean Connery* •439

I'm afraid the world has not seen a more completely non-golf person than myself. The game is an absolutely closed book to me and I would not even know which end to swing a caddie.

Denis Norden •440

Every rock 'n' roll band I know, guys with long hair and tattoos, plays golf now.

Alice Cooper, ageing rocker •441

I was three over: one over a house, one over a patio and one over a swimming pool. *George Brett* •442

Got more dirt than ball. Here we go again.

*Alan Shepard, Commander
of Apollo 14, playing golf
on his 1971 moon walk* •443

Golf is the only game where the worst player gets the best of it. He obtains more out of it as regards both exercise and enjoyment, for the good player gets worried over the slightest mistake, whereas the poor player makes too many mistakes to worry over them.

David Lloyd George •444

I like going there for golf. America is one vast golf course today. *Edward, Duke of Windsor, long after his abdication from the English throne* •445

Golf seems to me an arduous way to go for
a walk. I prefer to take the dogs out.

Princess Anne •446

Al Capone was not a particularly able golfer,
but he played honestly and with enjoyment.

New Yorker, 1937 •447

You have to let a little air into
the war room now and then.

Dwight Eisenhower •448

As General Eisenhower discovered, it is easier to
end the Cold War or stamp out poverty than to
master this devilish pastime.

James Reston •449

It is true that my predecessor did not object,
as I do, to pictures of one's golf skill in action.
But neither, on the other hand, did he ever bean
a Secret Servicemen. *John F. Kennedy, after an errant
drive hit one of his security officers* •450

One lesson you'd better learn if you want to be in
politics is that you never go out on a golf course
and beat the President. *Lyndon B. Johnson* •451

I would like to deny all allegations
by Bob Hope that during my last
game of golf, I hit an eagle, a birdie,
an elk and a moose. *Former US President Gerald Ford* •452

I know I am getting better at golf
because I'm hitting fewer spectators.

Gerald Ford •453

He'd rather face Congress than a three foot putt.

Ken Rayner on George Bush snr •454

Old, stupid, Bolshevik dressing,
pinchy-faced, golfing, bad-hair-day
people. I can't bear Republicans.

Cher •455

It took me seventeen years
to get 3,000 hits in baseball.
I did it in one afternoon on
the golf course.

Hank Aaron •456

Baseball reveals character; golf exposes it.

Ernie Banks •457

There's more tension in golf than in boxing because golfers bring it on themselves. It's silly really because it's not as if the golf ball is going to jump up and belt you on the whiskers, is it?

Henry Cooper •458

Golf is not a sport – it's an artistic exercise like ballet. You can be a fat slob and still play golf.

John McEnroe •459

Grass? Give me a bucket of balls and a sand wedge. Sure I like grass.

Ivan Lendl, a great tennis player who perennially struggled on grass courts •460

I've been playing until dark and even then I'm thinking about putting my car on the green so I can putt. *Ivan Lendl* •461

I'm actually a little nervous, like it's my first pro tournament. The first swing might be a little scary.

Tennis star, Jimmy Connors,
a good golfer, before a Pebble
Beach Pro-Am •462

We were on a nearby golf course when he suddenly changed direction unexpectedly in a golf cart. Obviously he's used to far greater speeds and I flew out of that cart like a projected missile – luckily I wasn't hurt at all.

Mark McNulty on playing golf with Nigel Mansell •463

The faraway bull in the field looks very small. But when it comes close you think, My God.

*Jose-Maria Olazabal approaches
a speech at the annual golf writers
dinner with more trepidation than
he ever approached a golf tournament.* •464

This speech is a bit like my tee shot.
I don't know where it's going.

*Jose-Maria goes for the cavalier
approach to public speaking* •465

Golf is a lot of walking, broken up by
disappointment and bad arithmetic.

unknown •466

By the time you get to your ball, if you don't know what to do with it, try another sport. *Julius Boros* •467

Lay off for three weeks and then quit for good.
Sam Snead dispenses advice to an incompetent pupil (attrib) •468

In case you don't know very much about the game of golf, a good one iron shot is about as easy to come by as an understanding wife. *Dan Jenkins wheels out the tired old wife gag* •469

Talking to a golf ball won't do you any good. Unless you do it while your opponent is teeing off.
Bruce Lansky •470

Never bet with anyone you meet on the first tee who has a deep suntan, a one iron in his bag, and squinty eyes.

Dave Marr •471

If you drink, don't drive. Don't even putt.

Dean Martin •472

Golf has taught me there is a connection between pleasure and pain. Golf spelt backwards is flog.

Phyllis Diller •473

One of the advantages bowling has over golf is that you very seldom lose a bowling ball.

Don Carter •474

A minute? I've got the whole damn weekend.

Fuzzy Zoeller, misses a cut and realises he has ample time for autograph hunters •475

The most exquisitely satisfying act in the world of golf is that of throwing a club. The full back-swing, the delayed wrist action, the flowing follow-through, followed by that unique whirring sound, reminiscent only of a passing flock of starlings, are without parallel in sport.

Henry Longhurst •476

Although golf was originally restricted to wealthy, overweight Protestants, today it is open to anyone who wears hideous clothing.
comedian Dave Barry •477

My God, it looks like a wax museum!
Former tour pro, George Low, attending his first seniors event •478

Years ago we discovered the exact point,
the dead centre of middle age. It occurs when
you're too young to take up golf
and too old to rush the net. *Franklin P. Adams* •479

Combination rest home and gold mine.
Dan Jenkins summarises the Senior Tour •480

We had one player drop out, one
transferred and one ran off with
Nick Faldo. *Rick La Rose sees his University
women's team decimated* •481

Give me the fresh air, a beautiful partner, and a nice round of golf and you can keep the fresh air and the round of golf. *Jack Benny* •482

Golf balls are attracted to water as unerringly as the eye of a middle-aged man to a female bosom

Michael Green in The Art Of Coarse Golf •483

Golf is like an 18-year-old girl with big boobs. You know it's wrong but you can't keep away from her.
Val Doonican •484

It's a bloody British invention for old ladies at golf clubs. *Australian, Peter Thomson, on foursomes* •485

When Langer practices on his own, he can hold up a fourball.
Dave Musgrove, Bernhard's long-time caddie •486

I've seen turtles move faster than Bernhard.
Lanny Wadkins, on Herr Langer •487

163

At his peak he was probably the best amateur golfer in the world despite a golf swing that, of his own admission, resembled a drunk shovelling coal.

Golf Journal, on Michael Bonallack •488

The number of shots taken by an opponent who is out of sight is equal to the square root of the sum of the number of curses heard plus the number of swishes. *Michael Green in* **The Art Of Coarse Golf** •489

American tourist, having just sliced his tee shot out of bounds:
In our country, we call that a Mulligan. What you call it over here?
St Andrew's caddie: A three.
Those Scots, you gotta love 'em •490

Rannulph Junuh: Anything else?

Bagger Vance: Just bash the living shit out of it.

> Matt Damon and Will Smith in
> *The Legend of Bagger Vance* •491

Why doesn't he just play the bloody game and leave the rest of us alone?

> *Alexander Walker reviews*
> *The Legend of Bagger Vance,*
> *Robert Redford's dire golf*
> *movie* •492

The world's number one tennis player spends 90% of his time winning, while the world's number one golfer spends 90% of his time losing. Golfers are great losers..•493

I play the game because my sole ambition is to do well enough to give it up. •494

The game is just a mirror, that's all it is. Your weaknesses glare you in the face. •495

I think I can win. I've got nothing better to do this weekend. *Feherty, before the 1994 Open Championship. He didn't* •496

Absolutely everyone has done it, but there are few people who admit it.

David Feherty, on choking •497

Hanging onto anxiety as if it were a family heirloom.

David Feherty, summed up by his psychologist, Alan Fine •498

I think I'll go cold turkey in the end and build golf courses. I'll torture other people. *David Feherty. He became a commentator instead.* •499

I was swinging like a toilet door on a prawn trawler.•500

168

I keep thinking that I might go out and play like Jack Nicklaus, but instead it's more like Jacques Tati. •501

I think the opportunities are vast off the course as well as on it. Besides, I've insulted everyone in Europe. *David Feherty, on his decision to live and work in the US* •502

Colin Montgomerie has a face like a warthog that has been stung by a wasp. •503

(It's) like one of those hot air hand dryers in toilets. It's a great idea and everybody uses it once, but never again. It takes too long. *David Feherty on Jack Nicklaus' Grand Cypress course in Florida* •504

The only time he opens his mouth is to change feet.

David Feherty on Nick Faldo •505

I don't know him but I've seen him smile and that's quite enough to put me off wanting to know anything about him.

David Feherty on Phil Mickelson •506

Worst haircut I've ever seen
in my life. And I've had a few
bad ones. It looks like he has
a divot over each ear.

David Feherty, on John Daly •507

I've noticed a lot of red
on putters these days: red
grips, red marks... this
one has a red neck.

David Feherty on
John Daly's putter •508

Don't worry, John. There are five courses out there. You're bound to hit one of them.

David Feherty to John Daly at St Andrews during the Dunhill Cup •509

It's not enough to have the skill to master
the course and beat the other players.
A golf champion needs to win the other
great battle, the internal one. The winner
is usually the player holding his or her nerve
over the last nine holes; the first three and a
half rounds just put them in with a chance.
And all the time the gurus lurk, waiting to
play with your head for their ten-per-cent.

They don't need to play their best golf to win. They only need to shoot the lowest score. *Rick Reilly, on what it takes to win* •510

Shoot a lower score than everybody else.

Ben Hogan divulges the secret of how to win the US open •511

Don't lose your temper about anything —
anything whatsoever. If you lose your temper,
you lose everything; self-control, self-respect,
judgment, equanimity, decency of language,
and of course, the hole, and probably the game.

Arnold Haultain, 1910 •512

Like pool, golf is primarily a game of position. The professional
pool player never takes one-shot at a time. He organises a series
of shots in his mind in order to sink all the balls on the table.
The key is to get a good leave or an ideal position for the next shot.

Course designer Robert Trent Jones •513

Prepare for success, accept what happens, then get ready for your next shot.

Davis Love III •514

If just some of the principles that keep players out of trouble in their day-to-day affairs were applied to their golf game, their handicaps would drop drastically. *Greg Norman* •515

If you can get the ball in the hole regularly by standing on your head, then keep right on, and don't ever listen to advice from anyone. *John Jacobs* •516

On the golf course you can't feel sorry for anybody. You have to try to win the golf tournament. You're not beating the guy you're playing against, you're beating the course. *Ernie Els* •517

Don't be in such a hurry. That little white ball isn't going to run away from you.

Patty Berg •518

Golf is not a game you can rush. For every stroke you try to force out of her, she is going to extract two strokes in return.

David Hill •519

With golf you can never get it right. If you work hard on the range to get things right, then you are automatically neglecting other things.

Nick Faldo, ever the perfectionist •520

Every great golfer has learnt to think positively. To assume the success and not the failure of a shot, to disregard misfortune and to accept disaster, and never to indulge the futility of remorse and blame. These are the hardest lessons of all.

Pat Ward-Thomas •521

When you go on that first tee and you're feeling bad, you know for sure that the guy you are playing is feeling just as bad.

Sam Torrance •522

When I'm in this state, everything is pure, vividly clear. I'm in a cocoon of concentration.

Tony Jacklin •523

When I'm in a zone, I don't think about the shot
or the wind or distance or the gallery or anything;
I just pull a club and swing. *Mark Calcavecchia* •524

Concentration is not an element that should be applied
all the way around a golf course. It is not the least bit
important until you're ready to shoot. There's plenty
of time to concentrate when you step up to the ball.

Julius Boros •525

The strategy of the golf course
is the soul of the game. The spirit
of golf is to dare a hazard, and
by negotiating it reap a reward.

George C. Thomas jr •526

When facing a hazard, focus
your attention sharply on
your target, not the hazard.

Bob Rotella •527

179

You play your best golf by just reacting to the target. If you are focused on the target, you aren't thinking about anything bad happening.

Davis Love III •528

Everyone has his own choking level, a level at which he fails to play his normal golf. As you get more experienced, your choking level rises.

Johnny Miller •529

If you need par, go for a birdie, because if you don't get the birdie you should hopefully get the par. *Nick Faldo* •530

I'll never forget that day. What I can't remember is how I did it.

Jose Maria Olazabal, trying to recall a remarkable 61 at the Firestone Club •531

There was an emptiness after I won
the Open. I'd worked so hard that
I couldn't imagine why I didn't feel
more overwhelmed. Later I realised
it is the doing that is the achievement,
not the winning. *Carol Mann* •532

Fourteen strokes.

*Hubert Green's succinct
summary of the difference
between an opening-day
81 and a second day 67* •533

Golf is the hardest game in the world. There's no way you could ever get it. Just when you think you do, the game jumps up and puts you in your place.

Ben Crenshaw •534

Pain and suffering are inevitable in our lives, but misery is an option.

Chip Beck •535

I accept the fact that I'm going to miss it sometimes. I just hope I miss it where I can find it.

Fuzzy Zoeller •536

The toughest thing for most people to learn in golf is to accept bad holes – and then forget about them. *Gary Player* •537

My worst day on the golf course still beats my best day at the office.

John Hallisey •538

If I can hit a curve ball, why can't I hit a ball that is standing still on a course?

Larry Nelson •539

If you screw up, you screw up. Nobody ever put an arm around my shoulder and guided me through the minefield.

Nick Faldo •540

The terrible thing about a missed shot in golf is that the thing is done, irrevocably, irretrievably. Perhaps that is why golf is so great a game; it is so much like the game of life. We don't have the shots over in either. *O.B. Keeler, US sportswriter* •541

A lot of guys who've never choked have never been in a position to do so. *Tom Watson* •542

I think I'll go to Hertz and see if I can rent a game.

*an out-of-form
Phil Rodgers* •543

What's the penalty for killing a photographer – one stroke or two?

Davis Love III •544

I want a ruling. I want to know which club to hit this guy with.

Hubert Green. The television vehicle had just run over his ball. •545

Lie? I've got no effing lie. I don't even
have an effing shot! *Miller Barber explains his*
lie to a TV commentator •546

If I had been in the gallery, I'd have gone home. *Johnny Miller, on his display on the front nine of a tournament* •547

I've had a bad week. But in the real world,
having a bad week is waking up and
finding you're steelworker in Scunthorpe.

Nick Faldo, after a poor Ryder Cup 1991 •548

If we can't beat Paraguay we might as well go home.
Colin Montgomerie at the 1993 Alfred Dunhill Cup. Cheerio, Monty •549

The Far Eastern countries have improved dramatically over the last ten
years. They can compete as well as anyone and proved that today.

This time, 1998, it is China who send
Monty and Scotland packing •550

There is no surer or more painful
way to learn a rule than to be
penalised once for breaking it.

Tom Watson •551

I give you one job to do and
you can't even get that right.

*Ian Woosnam, after incurring
a two-stroke penalty because
his caddie packed one club too
many at the 2001 British Open.
It cost him the lead, and possibly
the championship.* •552

The challenger was about to play his fourth shot towards the
green when across his line of play casually wandered a cow
and calf … he stopped and asked permission from his
opponent to move the object, as laid down quite clearly in
rule II. The reply came: the cow alone but not her offspring
– it is still growing.

H.M. Dixon •553

It is too much to ask a man to check his card for errors in arithmetic which his marker may inadvertently have made. It also points out a sorry weakness in the rules of the game that appoints a marker to keep score but doesn't make him responsible for its accuracy. *Peter Thomson, after Guy Wolstenholme suffers for someone else's mistake* •554

This is by far my worst experience in golf. Our whole team is disgusted. We all ask ourselves, is this how badly they want to win the cup? I thought it was an embarrassment.

Annika Sorenstam. She holed a chip in the 2,000 Solheim Cup, and her opponents insisted the shot be replayed, claiming she had played out of turn. •555

Madam, I'd like to look in your handbag. *Bob Shearer, forced to abandon etiquette after a female spectator pocketed his ball* •556

If you want to say something to me, say it after
the round when I can do something about it.

Greg Norman gets mean and moody with a spectator •557

I don't believe in jinxes. You control your
own ability and what other people do is
beyond your control. *Greg Norman at the*
1990 Masters. He
missed the cut. •558

I started in a Rolls-Royce
and ended up on a donkey.

Gordon Brand Junior lets
slip a six stroke lead •559

My kids used to come up to me and say: "Daddy, did you win?"
Now they say, "Daddy, did you make the cut?"

Tom Watson •560

I think every good man is tested
in the crucible of humiliation.

*Chip Beck manfully looks
for a positive after a 9&8
thrashing from Seve* •561

I should be standing up, my arse hurts so much.

*Jose-Maria Olazabal, after
a similar 8&7 tanking
from Ian Woosnam* •562

You get to know more of the character of a man in a round of golf than in six months of political experience.

David Lloyd George •563

I can tell right away if a guy is a winner or a loser just by the way he conducts himself on the course. *Donald Trump* •564

The most advanced medical brains in the universe have yet to discover the way for a man to relax himself, and looking at a golf ball is not the cure.

Milton Gross •565

You must attain a neurological and biological serenity in chaos. You cannot let yourself be sabotaged by adrenaline.
Mac O'Grady •566

I know of no better cure for illusions of grandeur than the game of golf.
Dr Beran Wolfe •567

Golf is a game in which perfection stays just out of reach. *Betsy Rawls, LPGA pro* •568

Although golf is a game played with other people, it is essentially an individualistic, and therefore a lonely experience. *Dr David Morely* •569

Golf is a spiritual game. It's like Zen. You have to let your mind take over.
Amy Alcott, LPGA pro •570

If you think positively and keep your mind on what is right, it gives you a better attitude. If you moan and groan and are disgusted, you play miserably too.

Bernhard Langer •571

I'm about five inches from being an outstanding golfer. That's the distance my left ear is from my right. Ben Crenshaw •572

Confidence is everything. From there, it's a small step to winning. Craig Stadler •573

Your ego is everything. And if you don't get that pumped up regularly, you can't last.

Dave Marr •574

I've learned that the more you play with the top players, the more you realise how many bad shots they hit. They're only human too. *David Gilford, on learning how to handle the big boys* •575

I had to figure out myself to figure out my game.

Stewart Cink •576

Golf is the most rugged, individualist sport there is. Of all athletes, golfers may most properly be able to have said I did it my way. There are no teammates to cover mistakes, no referees to monitor the games. There is a pact between sport and man. *Jim Murray* •577

After you get the basics down, it's all mental.

Ken Venturi •578

It doesn't much matter what kind of a club head is on one end of that shiny metal shaft if a fathead is on the other. *Robinson Murray* •579

You can get close enough to mastering the game, to feel it, to breathe it, maybe to smell it. But you can't master it, not for a long time. *Tom Watson* •580

Golf puts a man's character on the anvil, and his richest qualities – patience, poise, restraint – to the flame. *Billy Casper* •581

The more you miss, the worse it gets. The worse it gets, the more likely you are to miss again. *Dave Pelz* •582

A golfer doesn't know how well he can play until he wins one of the big tournaments under pressure.

Gay Brewer •583

Of all the games in which the soul of the Anglo-Saxon delights, there is perhaps none which is a severer test of that mysterious quality called nerve than the game of golf. *Horace Hutchinson* •584

I became the best in the world and I thought I had to change everything to stay the best. I tried to change my swing and that was a load of rubbish. I went to a sports psychologist and that was a load of crap. I'm a natural. *Ian Woosnam, on his failure to maintain the form that saw him win the US Masters* •585

I've never had a coach… Most people make everything far too complicated, in life as well as golf. You can pick up a club and just get on with it. *Laura Davies* •586

Parasites. Everything that needs to be said about the mental side of golf could be written on a single sheet of paper. *Mark James, on golf psychologists* •587

I began to realise I would never be a great tournament player. I didn't have the temperament. I lacked the guts or the nerve, call it what you like. Whenever I had the chance to win I would invariably lose. *John Jacobs, on why he turned to coaching* •588

Golf tips are like aspirin. One may do you good, but if you swallow the whole bottle you will be lucky to survive.

Harvey Penick •589

Golf has probably kept more people sane than psychiatrists have.

Harvey Penick •590

In golf your strengths and weaknesses will always be there. If you could improve your weaknesses, you would improve your game. The irony is that most people prefer to practice their strengths. *Harvey Penick* •591

Thinking must be the hardest thing we do in golf, because we do so little of it.

Harvey Penick •592

Never try a shot you haven't practised.

Harvey Penick •593

Practice is not to take the place of teaching, but to make teaching worthwhile.

Harvey Penick •594

Instead of putting pressure on myself and thinking, "I've got to make this shot", I just thought, "Go ahead and make it". It's a subtle difference but a big one.

Corey Pavin, on holing a nine iron in the 1993 Ryder Cup •595

If you're going to be a victim of the first few holes, you don't have a prayer. You're like a puppet. You let the first few holes jerk your strings and tell you how you're going to feel and how you're going to think. *Bob Rotella* •596

Golf is a game you never can get too good in. You can improve, but you can never get to where you master the game. *Gay Brewer* •597

I like to come from behind because I can play aggressively and go for broke. I have nothing to lose. *Karrie Webb* •598

I don't think people appreciate how hard we work, and mentally how hard it is to win a major. *Nick Faldo* •599

198

Don't ever call anyone Mister who
you may one day have to play.

Ben Hogan to Dave Marr •600

I played crap, he played
crap. He just out-crapped me.

*Wayne Grady, with a summary only an Australian
could give after losing the 1990 World Matchplay
championship to Greg Norman* 601

Papa, trust your swing.

*Note pinned to Vijay Singh's golf
bag during the 2000 US Masters.
It was written by his 10-year-old
son. He did, and he won.* •602

I have always believed there are far too many rules in golf. For me, if you cannot write them all on the back of a matchbox then something is wrong. *Henry Longhurst* •603

It is almost impossible to remember how tragic a place the world is when one is playing golf. Robert Lynd •604

Golf is a game to teach you about the messages from within, about the subtle voices of the body-mind. And once you understand them you can more clearly see your hamaratia, the ways in which your approach to the game reflects your entire life. Nowhere does a man go so naked.

Michael Murphy •605

Golf is the cruellest of sports. Like life, it's unfair. It's a harlot, a trollop. It leads you on. It never lives up to its promises. It's not a sport, it's bondage. An obsession. A boulevard of broken dreams. It plays with men. And runs off with the butcher. *Jim Murray* •606

It is a sport in which the whole American family can participate – fathers and mothers, sons and daughters alike. It offers healthy respite from daily toil, refreshment of body and mind. *Dwight Eisenhower* •607

It is impossible to imagine Goethe or Beethoven being good at billiards or golf.

H.L. Mencken •608

Human nature is so funny, it is a thousand pities that neither Aristotle nor Shakespeare was a golfer. There is no game that strips the soul so naked.

Horace Hutchinson, 1901 •609

The average player would rather play than watch. Those who don't play can't possibly appreciate the subtleties of the game. Trying to get their attention with golf is like selling Shakespeare in the neighbourhood saloon.

Bob Toski •610

Golf was never meant to be an exact science; it's an art form. Einstein was a great scientist but a lousy golfer.

Bob Toski •611

The golfer is Don Quixote attacking a windmill, a windmill that is literally, and by the way, figuratively, himself.

Al Barkow •612

Golf is an indispensable adjunct to high civilisation.

Andrew Carnegie •613

The Scots say that nature itself dictated that golf should be played by the seashore. Rather, the Scots saw in the eroded seacoasts the cheap battleground on which they could whip their fellow men in a game based on the Calvinist doctrine that man is meant to suffer here below and never more than when he goes out to enjoy himself. *Alistair Cooke* •614

When a man stands alone on the tee, surrounded by galleries he knows hold him in awe because of his talent at the bewildering game of golf and also because of his willingness to risk abject failure right out in the open, he very easily, very naturally sees himself as a hero figure.

Al Barkow •615

For an American of a certain age, cultural outlook and political inclination, a love of golf is more than faintly embarrassing. Is there any sound more evocative of greedy Republican smugness than the sound of golf spikes on brick? *David Owen* •616

It's the most humbling sport ever. It's like a lousy lover. It's like some guy who's never there when you need him. Every once in awhile, he comes and makes you feel like heaven on earth. And then the moment you say, I really need this, he's gone.

Dinah Shore •617

The glorious thing is that thousands of golfers, in parkland, on windy downs, in gorse, in heather, by the many sounding seas, enjoy their imbecilities, revel in their infirmities, and from failure itself draw that final victory – the triumph of hope.

R.C. Robertson Glasgow gets a bit carried away •618

Golf is to me what his Sabine farm was to Horace; a solace and an inspiration.

Ramsay MacDonald •619

Golf is an artist's game, it's a palette full of dewy grass and azure sky and well-raked bunkers. It is a philosopher's game, engaging wind and water to play strategic tricks on our concentration. And it is a gambler's game, asking us whether it will be the nerve to aim for the flag stick or the caution to settle for a probable bogey. *Reg Murphy* •620

Golf is a game which brings out the peculiarities and idiosyncrasies of human nature. It permits no compromises, recognises no weaknesses and punishes the foolhardy. Yet the apparent simplicity involved in hitting a small white ball from A to B lures all potential golfers into a false sense of security. Every instinct in the human psyche says the game looks easy,therefore it must be. That, for many of us, is where the trouble starts.

A.J. Dalconen •621

The number 18 is symbolically meaningful because it is the numerical equivalent of the Hebrew word chai, which means life. *Michael Bamberger, talking nonsense in his book To the Links Land* •622

The formula for par golf depends on three main factors, viz; Practice, Automatism and Reason (devoid of temperamental and other mental divergence), and the formula itself would be P+A+R=PAR. *Theodore Hyslop talking gobbledygook in 1927* •623

Golf is neither a microcosm of nor a metaphor for life. It is a sport, a bloodless sport if you don't count ulcers.

Dick Schaap •624

The "greatest player never to win a major" tag has hung like an albatross around the neck of some fine players; Tom Kite, Greg Norman and Phil Mickelson all suffered a number of near-misses before they struck gold. Colin Montgomerie is probably the finest player never to have won a Major, although Monty's formidable Ryder Cup exploits at least guarantee him a legacy.

There are so many good golfers today, it's an achievement to get a tour card, never mind win. A fine crop of European men and Asian women mean the Americans are not having things their own way for once.

If you don't get goosebumps when you walk into this place, you don't have a pulse.

Hal Sutton,
on Augusta •625

Augusta National is a young man's golf course, and you really need a young man's nerves to play on it.

Jack Nicklaus •626

208

It's like a black widow.
It seduces you, entices
you, romances you
— and then it stings you,
kills you emotionally.

*Mac O'Grady, on
Augusta National* •627

The course is perfection, and it asks perfection.

Nick Faldo, on Augusta National •628

If you have an ego of any sort, this course
will take it and shove it down your throat.

Tom Watson on Augusta National •629

How do I combat it? Just pray a little bit, I suppose.

Mark O'Meara on the par three 12th at Augusta National •630

Amen Corner looks like something that fell from heaven, but it plays like something straight out of hell.

Gary Van Sickle, on the tough sequence of holes around the turn at Augusta •631

These greens are so fast they must bikini wax them.

Gary McCord, on Augusta •632

Like playing a Salvador Dali landscape. I expected the clock to fall out of the trees and hit me in the face.

David Feherty, on Augusta National •633

I'm glad I brought this course, this monster, to its knees.

Ben Hogan, Masters winner in 1951 •634

So many people have come to me since I made that shot, to tell me they saw it. No golf course could hold that many people. *Gene Sarazen, on a famous eagle on the 15th at Augusta* •635

I've never been to heaven, and thinking back on my life, I probably won't get a chance to go. I guess the Masters is as close as I'm going to get. *Fuzzy Zoeller, winner in 1979* •636

He could be the first player to win the Masters who doesn't shave.

Paul Azinger on Tiger Woods in 1997. Tiger did win, aged 21. •637

Losing this Masters is not the end of the world. I let this one get away, but I still have a pretty good life. I'll wake up tomorrow still breathing, I hope.

Greg Norman, after losing a six stroke lead in the 1996 Masters •638

I don't know what to say. I just want to give you a hug.

Nick Faldo to Greg Norman, at the end of the 1996 US Masters. Faldo made up six shots over the last round. •639

Hey, Woosnam! This isn't some links course. You're at Augusta now.

Spectator to Ian Woosnam at the 1991 Masters. Woosie obviously appreciated the advice; he won. •640

Be patient. You know exactly how to play this course. You are the greatest golfer in the world.

The wording of a note given to Jose-Maria Olazabal in 1994, before the final round of the Masters. It was from his countryman and friend, Seve Ballesteros. •641

I made that putt. It just didn't go in.

Tom Kite, after missing on the final green in the 1986 Masters •642

Let's go home and hide some Easter eggs.

Greg Norman doesn't fancy hanging around after missing the cut at the Masters •643

I kept saying to myself all day that this would be my day. *Phil Mickelson finally delivers at the 2004 Masters* •644

I'm not going to say Phil hasn't taken the jacket off, but I know he slept in it. *Tina Mickelson* •645

The last year's champion serves as the host. He chooses the menu and picks up the tab. When I discovered that the cost of the dinner was more than the prizemoney, I finished second four times. *Ben Hogan, on the traditional Masters dinner* •646

I don't care about that. The Green Coat is enough for anybody.

Billy Casper expresses indifference to his fee for winning the Masters •647

Here's a simple way to abolish golf's elitist and exclusionary image and make it a truly all-American sport: ditch that fifties, Republican, martini-drinkers, green Brooks Brothers style sports jacket and make the winner of the Masters slip on something in, say, black leather with plenty of metal studs.

Bruce McCall, The Case Against Golf •648

There's one mistake in the drawing.
Hogan's in the trees and I'm on the fairway.

Billy Casper comments on a painting featuring
past Masters champions •649

The Masters is more like a vast Edwardian garden party than a golf tournament.

Alistair Cooke •650

I had a good chance to get in the Masters if I finished good.
And I was going good. Suddenly I was intercepted by five white
men who started following me around the course. They threw
their beer cans at me and called me nigger and other names.
This went on for several holes and the men were finally arrested,
but [only] after I lost a lot of strokes and finished far down the
list. *Charlie Sifford, 1959. Nearly 40 years on, Tiger Woods*
still experienced hostility at Augusta National •651

It's my favourite colour. I thought I'd let you fellows see me in it before Sunday.

Lee Elder, the first black golfer to play at Augusta National,
turns up wearing the club green. •652

I won three times and I never even got an outhouse.

Jimmy Demaret, three-time Masters winner. Gene Sarazen and Byron Nelson have bridges named after them at Augusta National •653

I don't visualise us having the Pizza Hut Masters.

Chairman of Augusta National, Hord Hardin, rejects the notion of sponsorship •654

How's my name going to fit on that thing?
Mark Calcavecchia, on the challenge presented to the engraver of the Claret Jug, after he won the 1989 British Open •655

I didn't think I should get away with it among so many fine young players. *A typically modest Henry Cotton wins the British Open in 1948, aged 41 •656*

The cigarette is tossed away, the club taken with abrupt decision, the glorious swing flashes and a long iron pierces the wind like an arrow. *Pat Ward-Thomas on Ben Hogan at the 1953 Open •657*

Keeping his wrists unbroken and moving the club head more slowly under pressure than the game's case hardened chroniclers had ever seen, Charles dropped putt after putt from any distance. *John Thicknesse watching Bob Charles win the 1963 British Open •658*

216

I said to myself, "this is getting silly. Don't stop".

Christie O'Connor jnr. He scored seven consecutive
birdies during a round of 64 at the 1985 British Open •659

To me, the Open is the tournament I would come to if I had to leave a month before and swim over. Lee Trevino •660

If you're going to be a player people will remember, you have to win the Open at St Andrews. *Jack Nicklaus* •661

I think, at that time, I'd always loved golf, but now it was a new type of love that I could have. *Tom Watson,*
recalling his win in the 1977 British Open •662

I'm not feeling down. If I'd played badly I might be. But when you are beaten by somebody, especially the way he played, you bow out gracefully. It was such a thrill to play to this standard of golf.

Nick Price after losing a thrilling tussle with Seve at the 1988 British Open •663

Just to play… is great. To do well in it is fantastic. To win it is a dream.

Ian Baker-Finch, British Open winner, 1991 •664

What now, I remember thinking, thunderbolts striking? There I am at St Andrews, playing with the king and I knock it out of bounds at the first. That was tough. *An out of form Ian Baker-Finch, paired with Arnold Palmer at the 1995 British Open* •665

It's hard to watch what he's going through. I know it is harder for him than us but, shit, it's still hard to watch. *Wayne Grady on the struggles of Baker-Finch* •666

Nothing compares to the Open. When you are handed that trophy the goosebumps stand up on the back of your neck looking at the list of previous winners.

Sandy Lyle defends the preeminence of the British Open •667

I never looked at the leaderboard all day. I had to play my own game. There was no point in looking, I can't alter anything out there.

Nick Faldo after his last, winning round at the 1987 British Open •668

It was straight at the flag, and I wanted to shout, cor, look at that. I went hot and cold all at the same time and then it was all over. *Nick Faldo, on his approach to the final green at Muirfield in 1987, when he won his first major* •669

Oh dear, oh dear. He's going in.

Peter Alliss, as Jean Van de Velde throws away the 1999 British Open by trying to play from the brook at the final hole •670

It was definitely slipping away from me. I've been after this for 10 years and I think if I didn't make it at this one, I never would have. *Ernie Els, British Open winner in 2002* •671

There are 150 people here, nobody saw it, nobody heard it – it wouldn't happen to f***ing Tiger Woods.

Gary Evans loses his ball on the 71st hole of the 2002 British Open. It cost him a place in the play-off for the championship. •672

I was distracted by Jesper Parnevik's outfit. I simply couldn't believe the colour of his trousers. *Mark Roe explains how he came to sign the wrong card in the 2003 British Open* •673

I just felt so proud to win the Open Championship. This is the Olympics of golf, the oldest and biggest of the majors. But even then it took a while to sink in.

Tom Lehman shows exemplary respect for the Claret Jug •674

This week it's a different style of golf, a style that I don't mind playing. I enjoy playing 'ugly golf', as I like to call it.

Todd Hamilton, winner of the 2004 British Open •675

One of the prerequisites to win a major championship is to enter the damn thing. You're not going to win the British Open by correspondence.

Tom Kite, in a sideswipe at US players who can't be bothered to play the British Open •676

While PGA touring professionals have been brought up on manicured courses since junior golf, the foreign contingent have been raised on bad lies and rough weather requiring mental toughness.

Pete Dye, during an era when non-American players were winning most of the majors •677

More money. Otherwise, no difference. Birdie the same. Par the same. Bogey the same. Out-of-bounds the same. *Seve Ballesteros, on the difference between the US tour and the European tour* •678

European courses require more imagination and that's why our tour has more character. *Nick Faldo* •679

On the European tour of the early 1980s we didn't play for a lot of money. We played just to win – all of us. We played purely to beat each other. *Nick Faldo* •680

In a major championship you don't care about the money. You're just trying to get your name on a piece of silver. *Nick Faldo* •681

Victory is everything. You can spend the money, but you can never spend the memories.

Ken Venturi •682

Let's see, I think right now I'm third in the money winning first in money spending.

'Champagne' Tony Lema •683

I made $700 for winning my first US Open and $500 for the British Open. Today a good, young golfer doesn't have to be champion. He gets $150,000 for wearing a logo on his cap or his sleeve. *Gary Player takes a dim view of sponsorship and endorsement fees •684*

You know, someday somebody's gonna come out here and tee it up nude.
Bob Wynn also takes a dim view of sponsorship and endorsement fees •685

I just don't think we should be classed alongside the dogs and horses.
Greg Norman disapproves of gambling on golf tournaments •686

Every kid learning to play golf dreams about winning the Masters, about winning the Open, not about being the leading money winner.

Tom Kite •687

To be truthful I think golfers are overpaid.
It's unreal, and I have trouble dealing with
the guilt sometimes. *Colin Montgomerie* •688

No tournament owes me anything.
I have to go out and earn it.
Colin Montgomerie •689

It looks like we are the average workers
and he is the gifted one. He doesn't practise
much. He doesn't need much practice.
Jose-Maria Olazabal on Colin Montgomerie •690

It's a lovely feeling to have whacked Monty. He's a
good friend but he's the last man you want
breathing down your neck in a tight situation.
When he gets the bit between his teeth he's
hard to beat. *Frank Nobilo takes pride in
holding Montgomerie at bay* •691

The Scot pulled his tee peg from the ground and, this time getting the yardage exactly right, bounced it neatly off the top of his tormentor's head.

*Martin Johnson, in the **Daily Telegraph**, on Monty's response to the perennial hecklers at the 2001 US Open* •692

The fact that I didn't win an eighth Order of Merit title was probably what saved my marriage. *Colin Montgomerie, in 2000. Sadly for Colin, the marriage would still fail.* •693

We were happily married for eight months. Unfortunately, we were married for four and half years.

Nick Faldo, on his personal problems •694

Before I won the Open, Christine and I had no problems at all but the publicity after that was colossal. Everybody wanted a bit of me. *Sandy Lyle on the pressures that broke up his first marriage* •695

I'll tell you what my life's like with Sandy; my wages must be the best on tour, and when I stay at his house at Wentworth he brings me to tea in the morning. That can't be bad, can it?

Dave Musgrove •696

I don't know what the plan is tonight, but I'm pretty sure I will be buying. *David Duval, after finishing top of the 1998 PGA money list* •697

On tour we get paid for performance.
If we don't play well, we're out of pocket.
If we get hurt and have to sit out a
season there's no income at all. *Tom Kite* •698

In Japan, player who scores hole-in-one while leading tournament always lose; it's proven jinx.

Ayako Okamoto •699

I looked down the list of competitors there and I was the only person I'd never heard of.

A starstruck Peter McEvoy at the 1978 World Series •700

It will take a plodder to win this championship. A player who plods on and on, the player to whom nothing much happens.

Colin Montgomerie at the 1993 US Open. It was won by Lee Janzen, who fitted the bill •701

Sometimes I wonder about practice. I've hit about 70,000 golf balls in the last four years, and some days I still play like an amateur. *Hubert Green* •702

When you finish second seven times in a season all sorts of terrible things go through your mind and that word choker would be top of the pile. You wonder if you will ever win, you wonder what you did wrong, whether it was your bad golf or someone else's brilliant golf. *Padraig Harrington after a happy end to a frustrating season in 2001* •703

For me, of course, winning at St Andrews was the last
ambition. I had won all the championships, they no longer
inspired me. *Michael Bonallack after victory in the Walker Cup in
1971 put the lid on his great amateur career* •704

Individually, they are pretty nice folks. But get them together
and they are about as miserable a bunch of people as you could
ever have the misfortune to run into in a supposedly civilised
world. *Tommy Bolt on British crowds.* •705

Right after I hit, some guy in the gallery yells out that I
was a wuss for laying up. I'm leading the tournament and
he's outside the ropes. Who understands better how to play
the hole? I have 13 years experience of when you lay up
and when you don't. I'm just not going to put up with it.
Davis Love III gets cranky about hecklers •706

Nothing changes. It's nice to come
back and see how bad greens can be.

Sergio García is scathing about the quality of European greens •707

I almost gave up golf in 1998. I had had injuries, I had lost my card. I had nowhere to play but invitations came in and it got me started again. I've won 10 times since '99

Michael Campbell after winning the 2005 US Open •708

It's the worst three putt in the history of golf.

Johnny Miller on Retief Goosen three-putting the last green at the 2001 US Open. Goosen came back the next day and won the play-off •709

It was possibly the most calamitous loss of nerve ever seen in a major championship. Never was a shorter, easier putt for a major championship missed.

David Davies in **The Guardian***, at the same event •710*

Stand them over an 18 inch putt to win a Major and the game reverts to its 15th century essence, the eternal puzzle of getting a little ball into a small hole.

Derek Lawrenson, the **The Daily Mail***, on the Goosen incident •711*

I noticed my name going up on the leaderboard. I got so excited I started making bogeys. By the time the scoreboard guys reached the 'y' in my name they were already taking down the 'D'. *Ed Dougherty* •712

I think he's just another person and not a particularly nice one at that. He certainly doesn't go out of his way to improve his image with other people. *Tony Jacklin on Ben Hogan* •713

It is like if I smash you very hard in the face four times a day, you do not like it very much. And if I smash you only once in the day, you say shit, this feels good! The pain I now have is heaven compared to what it was.

Jose-Maria Olazabal on pain management after his back injury •714

It's a torture chamber: if we had to play it every day I don't think I'd be playing golf. *Ian Woosnam on the pressures of tournament golf* •715

Without the people, I'd be playing in front of trees for a couple of hundred dollars.

Fuzzy Zoeller •716

He reminds me of a kid I used to play marbles with. When he couldn't win, he'd pick up his marbles and go home.

Dave Hill on Tom Weiskopf •717

I wouldn't mind if I was the next superstar. A lot of demands on your time then but I think I can put up with that.

Steve Stricker in 1996 •718

I hit a hook and went so far out of bounds I almost killed a horse in some stables a cab ride from the first fairway. I was so nervous I didn't have the strength to push the tee in the ground.

Mike Souchak, on his USPGA debut •719

We've lost our national way. We are a society of Chip Becks laying up intelligently. *Tom Callahan, in 1995, bemoaning the lack of adventure in modern American golf* •720

The way he talks, the way he walks, everything is so under control.

Justin Rose on Vijay Singh •721

I'm a golfer, not an athlete.

Lee Westwood •722

Golf, especially championship golf, isn't supposed to be any fun, was never meant to be fair, and never will make any sense. *Charles Price* •723

The first time I played here, back in 1959, I'll never forget it. People looked at me as if I had a tail.

Charlie Sifford, black PGA pro •724

Why are they picking on me? I'm just trying to make a living and I don't hurt anyone.

Charlie Sifford, after being heckled by racists in 1969 •725

This is my land. I am South African. And I must say now, and clearly, that I am of the South Africa Verwoert and apartheid. *Gary Player makes his position plain in 1966. His views would soften in later years.* •726

I do not believe in apartheid in sports and I have done many things trying to show that.

Gary Player in 1979 •727

Fifty years ago, a hundred white men chasing one black man across a field was called the Ku Klux Klan. Today it's called the PGA Tour.

(apocryphal) •728

234

Constitutionally and physically women are not fitted for golf. They will never last through two rounds of a long course in a day. Nor can they ever hope to defy the wind and weather encountered on our best links even in spring and summer. Temperamentally the strain will be too great for them.
Lord Wellwood, 1890 •729

We do not presume to dictate but must observe that the postures and gestures requisite for a full swing are not particularly graceful when the player is clad in female dress. *Lord Wellwood, 1890* •730

Women are admitted to play on the course only on sufferance and must at all times give way to members.
Royal St George's golf club, Kent •731

Trousers may be worn by women on the course, but must be taken off upon entering the clubhouse.

Golf club rule, 1927 •732

Let us examine the proposition that women golfers are people. It requires an effort to adjust to this idea, for ever since the beheading of the first woman golfer, Mary Queen of Scots, the golf world has openly regretted that the practice didn't start a trend.

Peter Dobereiner •733

Golf, I have been told, is physically a better game for our sex than any other, as it exercises a greater number of muscles without fear of overexertion or strain. *Issette Pearson, 1899* •734

I am a slave to golf.
Enid Wilson •735

I have never played golf with anyone, man or woman, amateur or professional who made me feel so utterly outclassed. *Bobby Jones on Joyce Wethered* •736

With wooden shafts you can stay on the ball longer. …you retained the feel longer. The ball didn't spring away from you.

Joyce Wethered •737

If the mind is full of fear or failure; a dread of the next approach, a persistent thought of three putts although the green is still far away, then, in my experience, there is but one thing that can at all help and that is to see the humour of the situation.

Joyce Wethered •738

A continental woman once showed up in black trousers – they were not called slacks then. We were shocked. I guess we were surprised and more scandalised.

Joyce Wethered, on women's course attire in the 1920's •739

I was young and righteous, but you cannot become a champion without the ability to cope with your emotions. *Mickey Wright* •740

I sometimes lose control of my emotions so completely, that I don't know where I am or that it's me hitting the ball. *Mickey Wright* •741

It was one of the greatest thrills of my life. I remember she was wearing tennis shoes and outdistancing the other ladies by 20 yards.
Paul Azinger, on caddying for Mickey Wright •742

Those were great times. Our purses were meagre by today's standards, but you could make a living of necessity, because we were always on the road and there were only a few dozen players. We were closer, too. After a tournament, we'd sit around together and have a party. Usually the winner would buy the drinks because she was the only one who had any money. *Kathy Whitworth, LPGA star* •743

She made women's golf. She put the hit in the swing.

Patty Berg on Babe Zaharias •744

You trying to ask me do I wear girdles and bras and the rest of that junk? What you think I am? A sissy?

Babe Zaharias •745

I just hitch up my girdle and let 'er fly.

Babe Zaharias. We thought you didn't wear one. •746

I don't know why you're practising so hard to finish second.

Babe Zaharias (attrib) •747

I would have worried if he didn't want a photograph.

Babe Zaharias thrives on attention •748

Babe Zaharias was a remarkable person… she definitely was stronger than most men. When she walked, the muscles rippled under her skin. She could hit it longer than I could, so could Mickey Wright. *Paul Runyon, a regular winner on the PGA Tour* •749

Is our organisation so unaware of the real glamour and attraction staring it in the face that it must resort to such trash? *LPGA pro Jane Blalock objects to the use of fellow pro Jan Stephenson as a pinup* •750

If I had legs like that, I'd pose that way too. Don't they have a Miss Piggy category?
Joanne Carner, on tour colleague Jan Stephenson's glamorous photos •751

Well it just goes to show what we've been saying all along. That all the good-looking golfers are on the ladies' tour.

Jan Stephenson, after a number of male golfers appeared in a Golf Magazine centrefold •752

As for my physical appearance, I am not a fashion model and have never pretended to be one. I am a professional golfer. But to be called a tank in print is very harsh. It isn't a nice way to wake up at 6:15 in the morning. *Laura Davies responds to some crass journalism* •753

There was one fan my caddy used to worry about. He would show up with a grocery bag. He would never come up and say anything to me. My caddie always wondered what the guy had in the bag, but he was harmless. *Jan Stephenson, the attractive Australian golfer, on the perils of scary stalker fans* •754

I wasn't feeling competitive the previous year; I was just playing golf and that's all.

Nancy López, on the need for a little bit extra •755

When we complain about conditions, we're just bitches. But when the men complain, people think, well, it really must be hard. *Betsy King* •756

The trouble with me is I think too much. I always said you have to be dumb to play good golf. *Joanne Carner* •757

I stayed in the bunker until I made one. They had to bring me cocktails and dinner.
Joanne Carner •758

I'm not concerned about getting in the record books. A good obituary doesn't exactly excite me. *Joanne Carner* •759

I thought you had to be dead to win that.

Joanne Carner, on being awarded the Bob Jones award for sportsmanship •759

I guess I'm not a professional's professional. I think I'd rather go to the dentist than play a practice round. *Laura Davies* •761

It took a gambling story to get me on the front page of the *The Daily Telegraph* when they had earlier hardly acknowledged the fact that I won my second major of the year. *Laura Davies* •762

As far as I'm concerned she is all mouth and no trousers.
Laura Davies takes exception to personal remarks by fellow pro Suzanne Pettersen •763

I showed up but my golf game didn't.

Beth Daniel •764

You could put any one of us on the European side and make it better. But the only Europeans who could help us are Laura Davies and Liselotte Neumann. *Beth Daniel is impressed with the US team at the 1992 Solheim cup. They lost.* •765

I cannot find a job that pays me £700,000 a year, so, until I do, I'll be right here. *Pat Bradley, LPGA pro* •766

I kept seeing her ass all day, bending over to pick her ball out of the hole.

Sally Little, after an awesome round by playing partner Hollis Stacey •767

If there is something to prove by all this, it is that your ordinary, everyday woman with a husband and kid can excel. *Judy Rankin, LPGA pro* •768

We'll either hire someone to travel with me or my Mom will do it. Just because you've had a baby doesn't mean you can't win tournaments. Nancy Lopez proved that.
Julie Inkster •769

I'm coming home and I'm bringing home the trophy and it's a big one.
Julie Inkster, 10 years later, having won the US Women's Open •770

I'll take a two shot penalty, but I'll be darned if I'm going to play the ball where it lies. *Elaine Johnson. She hit a tree, and the ball rebounded into her bra* •771

I've always been intense. I enjoy my job but it's a job.
Dottie Mochrie defends her unsmiling on-course demeanour •772

If golf was would-haves, could-haves and should-haves, I would have won everything by now.

Amy Alcott •773

When you're that young and everything is so new, you don't fear failure. If she knocks her putts by, she just makes them coming back. *Nancy López on Se Ri Pak* •774

I can't go out and party as much as I want. I have to behave. It's a big change for me and I'm doing it little by little.

Helen Alfredsson reluctantly introduces discipline into her life •775

They thought I was somebody just walking, hanging out in the rough.

Helen Alfredsson, at the 1994 US Women's Open, after a marshall tried to usher her off the course •776

Sometimes when a player makes it look as easy as she does, it's hard to appreciate how great she is.
Meg Mallon on Karrie Web •777

When she gets her game going, she's like a robot. She doesn't break down.
Beth Daniel on Annika Sorenstam •778

All you had to do was look at her. She has all the ability in the world. She can drive, chip, putt. All are shots of top-class. And the temperament. She is a high school Swede, one of the best talents in the world. *Laura Davies on Anika Sorenstam. Sorenstam has proved her right.* •779

This is a man's tour. There are guys out there trying to make a living. It's not a ladies' tour. If she wants to play, she should – or any other woman for that matter – if they want to play the man's tour, they should qualify and play like everybody else. *Vijay Singh on Anika Sorenstam's participation in a men's tour event* •780

I'm incensed by these guys. There are so few willing to be gentlemen about this. Here we have a woman willing to have a go at this, and the last athlete to deliberately put himself in this focus was Jesse Owens. She doesn't have to prove anything to me. She's the best woman ever to have played.
To have the guts to play the men and to endure this mean-spirited stuff, God Almighty, it's petty stuff. *David Feherty in defense of Sorenstam* •781

248

Good posture, chin up and then smile.

Yani Tseng reveals the positive attitude that helped her become the youngest player — male or female — to win a fifth Major when she lifted the Ladies British Open, aged 22, in 2011 •782

It doesn't matter how many Open championships or titles you may have won. When you stand on the tee at a Ryder Cup match and play for your country, your stomach rumbles like a kid turning up for his first tournament. *Arnold Palmer* •783

You have to remember that the Ryder Cup was the players' idea. It came from them. Even before Sam Ryder became involved we had played two matches between the professionals of the United States and Great Britain. *Gene Sarazen* •784

The format of the Ryder Cup was no doubt devised by somebody with a shrewd sense of the sadistic.

The Detroit News •785

If you like root canals and haemorrhoids, you'd love it there. *Nick Faldo on the Ryder Cup* •786

250

Stroke play is a better test of golf, but matchplay is a better test of character.

Joe Carr •787

Matchplay is so much more fun than strokeplay.
Sergio García •788

Don't tell the opponent to drive first when you have won the toss for the honour. It is a confession of weakness.
H. L. Fitzpatrick, 1900 •789

Never since the days of Caesar has the British nation been subjected to such humiliation.

Lord Northbourne, after Walter Travis became the first American to win the British amateur championship in 1904. We've got used to it. •790

On the sodden greens their approaches pitched past the pin, sat down and then, as a rabbit temporarily stunned, scuttled back, often fifteen feet before lying dead. *Leonard Crawley, in 1947, on the short iron play of the US Ryder Cup team* •791

We've had a great game, Arnold. Let's call it a half.
Peter Alliss plays the English gent at the 1961 Ryder Cup •792

I'll gladly tell you the message I've just given my boys in the locker room – and that is there aren't ten golfers from the whole world who could possibly beat us right now. *Arnold Palmer, US captain in 1963* •793

Ladies and gentlemen, may I present the finest golfers in the world.

Ben Hogan, US Ryder Cup captain, before the 1967 match •794

I didn't think you would miss it. But I wasn't going to give you the chance.

Jack Nicklaus at the 1969 Ryder Cup, conceding a missable putt to Tony Jacklin on the final green, thus halving their personal contest and the whole match. •795

The US players had worked their tails off to get into that position and then Nicklaus gave them a tie. I think most of the players were very upset. I would like to have seen Jacklin hole that putt and earn it outright. *Billy Casper is less magnanimous* •796

When it happened all the boys thought it was ridiculous to give him that putt. We went over there to win, not to be good ol' boys. I never would've given a putt like that – except maybe to my brother. *Sam Snead agrees with Casper* •797

I thank God I have this gift to play golf. I've come from nothing, eating from paper covered tables. This is our livelihood, were all tough pro's. I got shook up and I'm real sorry. *Ken Still, after a row with Brian Huggett and Bernard Gallacher in the 1969 Ryder Cup* •798

Can you imagine Jack getting beat by a guy smoking a pipe? *Arnold Palmer, on Brian Barnes. Jack was beaten twice in one day by Barnes in 1975.* •799

It's the comradeship, the friendships, the memories and experiences that count. It's not a bloody war! *Brian Barnes, 1975. The current crop would do well to remember that* •800

A tenacious little sod. All I had to do was my part because for sure he would do his. *Tony Jacklin on Brian Huggett, 1975* •801

In my first Ryder Cup match I played with Tommy Horton against Nicklaus and Watson a couple of months after Turnberry in 1977 and we held them to 5&4 We weren't intimidated but we had an inkling they might be slightly better than us. *Mark James* •802

254

I thought it was absolutely ludicrous dropping Tony from the
Ryder Cup team on the last day. He won the Open over that course.
*Peter Oosterhuis, after Jacklin was omitted from the singles
in the 1977 Ryder Cup* •803

We allowed ourselves to become intimidated by
American self-confidence. The main challenge
is one of psychology – breaking down the
European reserve and inferiority complexes
before we meet the millionaire superstars.

*Tony Jacklin, in 1983. It was two more years before the self
belief he instilled in the team bore fruit.* •804

Hang your egos outside, let's put this effort into the team.

Tony Jacklin, before the 1985 Ryder Cup •805

Before, when I played in the Ryder Cup it had been in the company of Watson and Nicklaus. You felt two down as soon as they walked into the same room. This time it was different. The Americans had nobody with that charisma.

Howard Clark, 1985 •806

To tell you the truth, I thought they were a bunch of cry babies and I told them that.

Lee Trevino, beaten US captain at the 1985 Ryder Cup •807

I meant to tell Lee Trevino not to be too despondent. This cup is going to change hands quite often in future. He will not be the last losing American captain.

Tony Jacklin, in 1985, rightly predicted a different pattern to the contests after years of American domination •808

If I were Europe I'd make him captain for the next thirty years. If they don't want him, give him to us. That man is a winner. *Peter Jacobsen on Tony Jacklin* •809

Losing the Ryder Cup did not bother me as much as the behaviour of the galleries. All that cheering when we missed shots. I've never known anything like it before and especially not from a British crowd. You expect so much from them. *Peter Jacobsen in 1985* •810

British golf galleries besmirched themselves last year when the Europeans defeated the United States in the Ryder Cup. Hal Sutton went back to the US and was devastated at the behaviour he had witnessed. *Greg Norman objects to partisanship on British courses* •811

They've won hundreds of tournaments and millions of dollars. Possibly they are helping each other out too much. They got where they are on their own.

Raymond Floyd 1989, on the U. S. players' perennial struggle in the team formats •812

All my players are seasoned campaigners. They have won tournaments and probably millions of dollars. But they feel like rookies when it comes to the Ryder Cup – even those who have played before.

Raymond Floyd in 1989, on the unique tension created by the Ryder Cup •813

You've got to know when it's time to say goodbye.

Tony Jacklin, relinquishing the Ryder Cup captaincy in 1989 •814

Perhaps we were too busy celebrating our home-grown championships
to care about this little international contest. But that has all changed.
We learned how much the Ryder Cup means once we had to fight for it.

*Ken Burger, 1991, on how parochialism has hampered the US
Ryder Cup performance* •815

You can be friendly with them another time. For one week we're trying to beat these guys.

*Raymond Floyd admonishes Fred Couples for applauding his
opponents' shots in the 1991 Ryder Cup. Couples was always
able to rise above the meanness of recent Ryder Cup fixtures.* •816

We made a mistake but we certainly aren't cheating.

Paul Azinger, after he and his partner infringed the rules at the 1991 Ryder Cup •817

It has nothing to do with cheating. Cheating
and breaking the rules are two different things.

Seve Ballesteros, who pointed out the infringement •818

No one in the world could have holed that. Jack Nicklaus wouldn't have holed it nor would Tony Jacklin. And I certainly wouldn't have holed it.

Seve on the putt missed by Bernard Langer
at the end of the 1991 Ryder Cup •819

American pride is back. We went over there and thumped the Iraqis. Now we've taken the cup back. I'm proud to be an American. *Paul Azinger after the 1991 Ryder Cup* •820

It was like that World Wrestling Federation stuff on television where you have bad guys and good guys — we were the bad guys. When the Americans apply themselves to winning something as seriously as they have the Ryder Cup, you know you have to cope with a very ruthless animal.

Bernard Gallacher on the shenanigans at Kiawah Island in 1991 •821

No matter how hard the press beat me up, I deserve it. They won't be any harder on me than I am on myself.

Curtis Strange, at the 1995 Ryder Cup, after losing the last two holes and his match to Nick Faldo •822

They inspired each other. There was a lot of Spanish pride too. So when you get such fierce pride and immense respect for each other, it can be a lethal cocktail. *Bernard Gallacher, on the Ryder Cup pairing of Seve Ballesteros and Jose-Maria Olazabal* •823

If they are going to make a twenty footer and we're going to miss an eight footer, what can you do?

Tom Kite 1997, on the failure of his big stars to deal with the pressure of the Ryder Cup •824

I'm still totally convinced we have the twelve best players, today proved that. But put their guys together and they have magic at their fingertips.

Tom Lehman, after a US comeback in the singles fails to stop Europe winning the 1997 Ryder Cup •825

I seem to be blamed for winning the Ryder Cup but
I had eleven very strong individuals with me as well.

*Colin Montgomerie, on being heckled by American fans
after the 1997 Ryder Cup* •826

We are playing for our souls.

Ben Crenshaw comes over all Faustian before the 1999 Ryder Cup •827

He's a huge inspiration to us.
We're lucky to have him on our side.
He's great with the crowd and great for
the game. *Colin Montgomerie on the precocious
Sergio García at the 1999 Ryder Cup* •828

The players look to Monty for inspiration
and leadership. He sets the tone, no question.

Mark James, 1999 •829

I have never been more scared in my life on a golf course than I was at Brookline. It was frightening to hear people shouting "kill, kill" and "bring out the body bags". *Ken Schofield, European tour director, on the 1999 Ryder Cup* •830

The most disgusting thing I've ever seen.

Sam Torrance on the notorious incident on the 17th green at Brookline •831

I felt embarrassed for golf. It went beyond the decency you associate with proper golf. I love the Ryder Cup and I don't want to see it degenerate into a modern demonstration every time we play. *Sir Michael Bonallack 1999* •832

I guess every story needs a villain and I'm glad he's found one in me. I hope he feels good about making money out of taking shots at other people's character and integrity.
Tom Lehman response to criticism from Mark James after the 1999 match •833

The Ryder Cup is an enormous moneymaker. Because of that, I think it's all right to give funds to help our communities.

Tiger Woods tries to justify asking for appearance money in the Ryder Cup •834

They're going to kick the crap out of the other guys. In the past, Europe have guys like Nick Faldo and Bernhard Langer who could really get after it. Now they've got Darren Clarke going down the fairway smoking a cigar.

Steve Elkington predicts a crushing the US victory at 2001 Ryder Cup. The cup was delayed for a year. Europe won. Clarke played well •835

I don't believe this is an appropriate time to play competitive golf. I feel strongly this is a time to pause, reflect and remember the victims.

Tiger Woods advocating the cancellation of the 2001 Ryder Cup. •836

The results of games should never matter too much. But if they don't matter at all nobody should bother to play. That surely is the case with the Ryder Cup.

Hugh McIlvanney, Sunday Times sports correspondent, agrees with Tiger •837

The physical and strategic complexity
of golf have always made it perfect fodder
for the sportswriters. The thin line between
success and failure lend a special tension,
and the slow pace of the game eliminates
hasty and hysterical writing. The same
tension offers TV dramatic opportunities
that more immediate sports lack. TV can
sometimes give an overview and a panorama
that on-course viewing lacks.

With reference to the reported world's record rebound of a golf ball from the head of the Scotch caddie which appeared in the home golfing papers, I beg to inform you that whilst playing the seventh hole of the Premier Mine course on 28th of September my ball struck a native caddie (who was standing 150 yards away at the side of a tree just off the line of the fairway) on the forehead just above the right eye. The drive in question was one of those so dear to a golfer, a hard raking shot. The ball, a colonel, rebounded back in a direct line 75 yards (distance measured). Strange to relate, but beyond a slight abrasion of the skin, the native was not affected at all.

A letter to **Golf Monthly** *from Edward Stanward in 1914*
(thanks to Dale Concannon's **Wise Words for Golfers***)* •838

Golf is a game to be played between cricket and death.

Colin Ingleby-McKenzie •839

I regard golf as an expensive way of playing marbles.

G K Chesterton •840

Golf is not a funeral, although both can be very sad affairs.

Bernard Darwin •841

Golf is like a love affair. If you don't take it seriously, it's no fun; if you do take it seriously, it breaks your heart. *Arnold Daley* •842

Golf is an open exhibition of overweening ambition, courage deflated by stupidity, skill soured by a whiff of arrogance.

Alistair Cooke •843

Golf is so popular simply because it is the best game in the world at which to be bad.

A. A. Milne •844

Golf is typical

If there is any larceny in a man, golf will bring it out.

Paul Gallico •846

No other game (lest it be polo) is as thoroughly associated with capitalism and its oppression as golf. *John Updike* •847

I'd played in three Ryder Cups before a golf writer even condescended to speak to me. Now they are giving press conferences twice a day.

Peter Alliss, for whom the grass will never be as green •848

Golf is a day spent in a round of strenuous idleness. *William Wordsworth* •849

Golf is a game in which you try to put a small ball in a small hole with implements singularly unsuited to the purpose.

Winston Churchill, attrib. •850

capitalist lunacy.

George Bernard Shaw •845

Golf… is the only game in the world in which a precise knowledge of the rules can win a reputation for bad sportsmanship. *Patrick Campbell* •851

"After all, golf is only a game", said Millicent.
Women say these things without thinking. It does
not mean that there is a kink in their character.
They simply don't realise what they are saying.

P.G.Wodehouse •852

Sudden success in golf is like the sudden acqui-
sition of wealth. It is apt to unsettle
and deteriorate the character. *P.G.Wodehouse* •853

There was the man who seemed to be attempting to
deceive his ball and lull it into a false sense of security by
looking away from it and then making a lightning slash in
the apparent hope of catching it off its guard.

P.G. Wodehouse •854

The least thing upset him on the links.
He missed short putts because of the uproar
of the butterflies in the adjoining meadows.

P. G. Wodehouse •855

The man who can go into a patch of rough alone with the knowledge that only God is watching him, and play his ball where it lies, is the man who will serve you faithfully and well. *P.G.Wodehouse* •856

The only way of really finding out a man's true character is to play golf with him. In no other walk of life does the cloven hoof so quickly display itself.

P. G. Wodehouse •857

Golf, like measles, should be caught young, for, if postponed to riper years, the results may be serious. *P.G.Wodehouse* •851

Golf is a game of such monumental stupidity that anyone with a brain more active than a cantaloupe has difficulty gearing down to its demands. *Peter Andrews* •859

Next time I come back as a golf writer. No three putts. Never miss a cut. And somebody else pays. *Roberto de Vicenzo* •860

When I started, the professional tour was like a travelling circus, a nomadic village. …but that is all gone and now even the community spirit among players is breaking down. *Peter Dobereiner* •861

These days I'm a columnist, a technical term meaning a writer who hides in the mountains during the heat of battle and then comes down to bayonet the wounded. *Peter Dobereiner* •862

Water creates a neurosis in golfers. The very thought of this harmless fluid robs them of their normal powers of rational thought, turns their legs to jelly, and produces a palsy of the upper limbs.

Peter Dobereiner •863

The professional golf watcher never catches the action. I could write a volume on Great Moments in Golf I Have Missed. *Peter Dobereiner* •864

272

Not a week goes by without my learning something new about golf. That means, of course, that I was ignorant of eight things about golf two months ago. Extend the process back nearly twenty years and the result is an impressive accumulation of ignorance. *Peter Dobereiner* •865

I never pray on a golf course. Actually, the Lord answers my prayers everywhere except on the course.
American evangelist preacher Rev Billy Graham •866

I won't try to describe AR's game, beyond saying the way he played it would have taken three years of solid practice to work up to where he could be called a duffer. *Paul Gallico* •867

Here were decent godless people: Their only monument the asphalt road And a thousand lost golf balls. *T.S. Eliot, from* **The Rock** •868

Like chasing a quinine pill around a cow pasture.

Winston Churchill summarises the game •869

Men who would face torture without a word become blasphemous at the short fourteenth. *A. P. Herbert* •870

The determining bulk of Scotch people had heard of golf ever since they had heard of God and often considered the two as of equal importance. *G. K. Chesterton* •871

They think nothing of walking right in for coffee. But they wouldn't dream of interrupting you at golf.

Harper Lee on folk in the southern states •872

Golf appeals to the idiot in us and the child. What child does not grasp the simple pleasure-principle of miniature golf? Just how childlike golf players become is proven by their frequent inability to count past five. *John Updike* •873

Class, someone once said, is the ability to undergo pressure with grace. So what did I do? I just did what comes naturally. I vomited.
Charles Price, on leading a golf tournament •874

A job into which men drift, since no properly constituted
parent would agree to his son starting his career in that way.
Bernard Darwin •875

This going to the nineteenth is an odious business.
It combines the excitement of the gaming table,
a duel and a Roman amphitheatre. *Bernard Darwin* •876

Who wants to know what Faulkner says? My readers want to read my view of things.

*Bernard Darwin turns his nose up at
the idea of a press conference in 1951* •877

I don't like watching golf on TV. I can't stand whispering.

Comedian David Brenner •878

Watching the Masters on CBS is like attending a church service. Announcers speak in hushed, pious tones, as if to convince us that something of great meaning and historical importance is taking place. What we are actually seeing is grown men hitting little balls with sticks. *Tom Gilmore* •879

Golfing excellence goes hand-in-hand with alcohol, as many an open and amateur champion has shown.

Henry Longhurst •880

Golf, perhaps through it's very slowness, can reach the most extraordinary heights of tenseness and drama. *Henry Longhurst* •881

Almost to a man America's indigenous golf commentators
sound like half-wit hillbillies reliving all their yesterday's round
a campfire. *Ian Wooldridge, British journalist* •882

If you want to take long walks, take long
walks. If you want to hit things with
sticks, hit things with sticks.
But there's no excuse for combining
the two and putting the results on TV.
National Lampoon •883

I don't think television work has screwed
up my golf. I've pretty much taken care of
that on my own. *Curtis Strange* •884

My career started slowly and then tapered off. *Gary McCord* •885

All games are silly, but golf, if you look at it dispassionately, goes to extremes. *Peter Alliss* •886

One is the complete golf professional and the other the complete professional golfer.

Peter Alliss enlightens us about the difference between Tom Watson and Brian Barnes •887

I extol not only the virtues but also the nonsense of the game; the silliness and bitchiness of it all. I mean all that these grown men are doing is knocking a ball round a beautiful place. Although these players think it's the real world, it's not.

Peter Alliss, who sees vanity in all but himself •888

It would be an act of unimaginable masochism to plough through a tape of Alliss commentary. *Marina Hyde, of The Guardian* •889

The Socrates of the snug bar.

The Evening Standard's Matt Norman on Peter Alliss •890

A bird flying to the firmaments outlined against an incandescent sky, begging to fall, sashaying gently back to the earth. *Mac O'Grady* •891

I don't go much for those in-depth interviews that want to know the colour of your curtains and how many times you make love to your wife.

Tom Watson, a shy and private man, in the The Daily Mail, 1982 •892

It's Monday, guys. Don't start overloading me on Monday. There're still two days of hype left.

Greg Norman encourages calm amongst the press before the 1989 US Masters •893

Azinger is wearing an all-black outfit: black jumper, blue trousers, white shoes and a pink tea cosy hat.

Renton Laidlaw has problems with his colour chart •894

The par here at Sunningdale is 70 and anything under that will be a score in the 60s. *Steve Rider* •895

Some weeks Nick likes to use Fanny, other weeks he prefers to do it by himself.

Ken Brown, on Nick Faldo's preference when lining up putts. Fanny Sunesson was Faldo's caddy at the time •896

I would like to thank the press from the heart of my bottom.

Nick Faldo in bitter mood after winning the 1992 British Open •897

Golf's three ugliest words: still your shot.

Dave Marr •898